Still Learning to Read

Still Learning to Read

Teaching Students in Grades 3–6

Franki Sibberson
Karen Szymusiak

Stenhouse Publishers
Portland, Maine

Stenhouse Publishers
www.stenhouse.com

Credits

Page 2: From *Junie B. Jones and the Stupid Smelly Bus* by Barbara Park, copyright © 1992 by Barbara Park. Used by permission of Random House Children's Books, a division of Random House, Inc.

Page 33: From *Kidbits* by Jenny Tesar, Blackbirch Press, © 1996, Blackbirch Press. Reprinted by permission of The Gale Group.

Page 41: "Confessions of a Reader" by Carol Wilcox is reprinted from *All That Matters: What Is It We Value in School and Beyond?* Edited by Linda Rief and Maureen Barbieri. Copyright © 1995 by Heinemann. Published by Heinemann, a division of Reed Elsevier, Inc., Portsmouth, NH. Reprinted by permission of the publisher.

Page 120: From *Mick Harte Was Here* by Barbara Park, copyright © 1995 by Barbara Park. Used by permission of Alfred A. Knopf, an imprint of Random House Children's Books, a division of Random House, Inc.

Pages 123, 128: From *Once Upon a Fairy Tale: Four Favorite Stories Retold by the Stars,* copyright © 2001, reprinted with permission of The Starbright Foundation.

Page 127: Text copyright © 2001 by Rebecca Kai Dotlich from *When Riddles Come Rumbling* by Rebecca Kai Dotlich. Published by Wordsong, Boyds Mills Press, Inc. Reprinted by permission.

Library of Congress Cataloging-in-Publication Data
Sibberson, Franki.
    Still learning to read : teaching students in grades 3–6 / Franki Sibberson, Karen Szymusiak.
        p. cm.
        Includes bibliographical references.
        ISBN 1-57110-359-7 (alk. paper)
        1. Reading (Elementary) I. Sibberson, Franki. II. Title.
LB1573.S99 2003
372.41—dc21   2003053909

Cover and interior design by Martha Drury
Cover and interior photography by Meredith Melragon

Manufactured in the United States of America on acid-free paper
09 08 07 06 05 04 9 8 7 6 5 4 3

For our good friend Louise Borden,
whose friendship is a celebration of literacy and learning

Contents

Acknowledgments

I've always depended on the conversations of others to bring my own thinking to light.
Dorothy Watson

Conversations have been the foundation for our own thinking and writing. The talk that surrounds our teaching and learning clarifies, strengthens, and extends our commitment to help our students become thoughtful readers. The conversations we have with children give us insight into the process of learning to read and connect us to our own reading experiences. Within our learning communities, conversations count.

We have been fortunate throughout our teaching lives to work with and learn from amazing people—Donna Barnes, Max Brand, Patty Carpenter, Ann Marie Corgill, Judy Davis, Ralph Fletcher, Molly Foglietti, Bob Griffith, Mary Lee Hahn, Stephanie Harvey, Shelley Harwayne, Ellin Keene, Debbie Miller, JoAnn Portalupi, Katie Wood Ray, Regie Routman, Joanne Hindley Salch, Sharon Taberski, and Cris Tovani. These people continue to inspire and support us.

For their leadership and commitment to our learning communities and to our work with children, we appreciate all those in the Dublin City Schools, especially Dan DeMatteis, Corrine Evans, Linda Fenner, Jill Reinhart, and Sharon Zimmers.

Franki would like to thank her students, the parents, and the staff at Eli Pinney Elementary School in Dublin, Ohio. Because of Tom Bates's leadership, the school is a great place for children and teachers. She is lucky to be a part of such an amazing community of learners. A special thank-you goes to Matt DeMatteis, Marie Sergio, Kevin Simmons, and Andrew Solveson.

Karen values the time she spends with the children, parents, teachers, and staff at Olde Sawmill Elementary School in Dublin, Ohio. It is what they accomplish together that makes their school a great place to learn. She considers herself fortunate to spend her days alongside children and to be part of their literate lives.

Meredith Melragon worked through her lunch hours to take the photos for the book. Because she understands teaching and learning so well, she was able to capture life in the classroom.

Without Sally Oddi, owner of Cover to Cover, our favorite children's bookstore, we would not be able to keep up with children's books the way that we do. We feel lucky to have such a great resource so close to home!

For making the book a reality, we appreciate everyone at Stenhouse who supported us along the way, especially Philippa Stratton, Tom Seavey, Martha Drury, and Emily Field.

Brenda Power understood and supported our unique writing habits. Besides being a brilliant editor, she has a great sense of humor that helped us to laugh when we really wanted to cry. She was especially wonderful during the home stretch.

Our families continue to support our work and our writing. They listened to us talk about our students, read drafts of the book, and took care of the house while we wrote. We could not have done it without them! Karen thanks her husband, Dave; her children, Zac and Amanda; and her parents, Angie and Ralph Jaworski. She also thanks her sisters, Linda Grasso and Jean Leach, and her brother, Ralph. Franki thanks her husband, Scott; her daughter, Alexa; and her parents, Pat and Cathy Agresta. She also thanks A. J., Susan, and Jaime.

While writing this book, we learned from the children who kept us grounded in what was real and ever-present in their reading lives. We continue to be amazed at their incredible thinking and insights. We are lucky to spend our days with children whose conversations bring our own thinking to light.

CHAPTER 1

Teaching Reading in the Upper Elementary Classroom

I've known how to read for almost four years now . . .
    Courtney

Early one year, we asked fourth graders to think about their growth as readers and to write about their reading lives. We smiled as we read Courtney's words, but they started us thinking. Courtney wrote, "I've known how to read for almost four years now . . ." Courtney was proud of how far she had come as a reader. In those four years, she had moved from being a nonreader to being a very good reader of many texts. However, we know that four years is only the beginning of her life as a reader. Courtney's comment reminds us that students in the upper elementary grades have not been reading for very long. We can't possibly expect them to have learned all that they need to know about understanding complex texts in such a short time.

Teachers in the upper elementary grades face realistic fears about the teaching of reading. First of all, many of us received relatively little training in how to teach reading. We might not feel as capable as primary teachers in this area. The public still believes that in grades K–2 we teach children how to read and in grades 3–6 our students read to learn. The implication is that at the upper elementary levels, time spent teaching children how to read is time not well spent. The assumption is that students in these grades should be focused on learning content—they should already know how to read.

Laura Robb (2002), in an article for *Scholastic Instructor,* questions our past practices and encourages us to rethink the teaching of reading in the upper elementary grades. "For years," she writes, "many elementary and middle school teachers have shaped their teaching practices around the deeply rooted myth of 'Learning to Read and Reading to Learn' . . . Although the myth and the practices associated with it do not by any means tell the entire reading story, they have influenced reading instruction in many classrooms for years. The problem? The myth and its practices aren't working. What many researchers have now shown is that for all children, learning to read and reading to learn should be happening simultaneously and continuously, from preschool through middle school—and perhaps beyond" (p. 23).

Our older readers still have much to learn about reading. It makes sense that students in grades 3–6 need more instruction. The texts they are reading are becoming much more complex and sophisticated. As readers, they will be asked to think through complex themes, analyze characters, and respond at higher levels. For these students to grow as readers, they need more instruction. We can't assume that the skills our students learned in grades K–2 will carry them through their lives as readers. They are ready for new skills and more independence.

As teachers of readers in the upper elementary grades, we have learned that students at this level can really benefit from our teaching skills and strategies they can use on their own as they read, rather than continuing to rely on adults to model and guide them through the reading process, as they have done in earlier grades.

Meeting New Challenges in Reading

The children who enter our classrooms have had support and instruction that built a foundation for their early reading experiences. They are accustomed to reading books that clearly build success for the reader from the first page on. Here, for example, is the start of *Junie B. Jones and the Stupid Smelly Bus,* a book for early readers, by Barbara Park.

> *My name is June B. Jones. The B stands for*
> *Beatrice. Except I don't like Beatrice. I just*
> *like B. and that's all.*
>> *I'm almost six years old.*
>> *Almost six is when you get to go to kindergarten.*
> *Kindergarten is where you go to meet new friends and*
> *not watch T.V.*
>> *My kindergarten is the afternoon kind.*
>> *Today was my first day of school. I'd been*
> *to my room before, though. Last week, Mother*
> *took me there to meet my teacher. (p. 1)*

It's easy for early readers to understand what they read because the framework for the story is clearly presented on the first page or two. But they meet new challenges in reading as they enter the upper elementary grades. The stories they read unfold more slowly, and readers need persistence and have to be comfortable with some ambiguity until the pieces of the story fit together. New complexities arise in nonfiction as well.

Last year, we worked with a small group of sixth-grade students. These children were having trouble choosing and sticking with books. We watched them, and we realized that they usually chose books by the cover illustration and the title. They didn't seem to know how else to preview a book for selection. So we led them through a preview of *Flying Solo* by Ralph Fletcher. This book is always a favorite with students in the upper elementary grades: it's a book about what sixth graders do on a day when the substitute teacher doesn't show up!

We asked the children to look at the title and illustration on the cover. Then we had them look at the blurb on the back of the book, the review excerpts they found there, and the first page of the story. They looked at each of these features one at a time and talked with us about what they learned from each. The students then began to piece together what they knew about the story before they began to read the book. After drawing their attention to each feature, we asked the children whether or not this looked like a book that would be interesting to them. After taking a look at the cover, all of the children decided they were eager to read the book. They remained eager to read the book after reading the blurb. They were even more anxious to read the book after having read the reviews. At this point, we expected that these students would be fighting over the few copies of *Flying Solo* that we had in the classroom.

But then the students read the first page with us. We were shocked: the entire group of children changed their minds and no longer seemed interested in *Flying Solo*. Rebecca suggested a teacher should read the book aloud to them instead and the others agreed. The whole group immediately shut down and was ready to abandon the book.

What had happened? We knew that the text wasn't too difficult and that the children had a good idea of what would happen in the story from the previewing we had done. So we talked for a while about what had changed their minds. After considerable discussion, we realized that the children had expected the substitute to be a no-show on the very first page of the story. When that didn't happen, they lost confidence, knowing that they would have to get past the "setup" in order to get to the "real story." It wasn't until page 26 when the students in *Flying Solo* realized they would be without a teacher for the day. Although the actual text level wasn't too hard for them, the nature of the first few chapters made the book difficult.

For these struggling readers, twenty-six pages was a *lot* of reading—far too much to "get through" before the story became exciting to them. They wanted to read the book, but they didn't have the stamina to read to page 26 on their own. A few students asked if they could just start reading on page 26. Others begged us to read the first twenty-five pages aloud to them. Because some of the students had not had many successful experiences with reading, they didn't have enough trust in books to know that what they read on the first twenty-six pages would be critical throughout the story. These children were reading the Junie B. Jones books just a few years earlier. Books like the ones in the Junie B. Jones series set up the entire story on the first page. Students who are accustomed to reading books that set up the story on the first page are confused and frustrated when the first page of a book does not do that. They need instruction to learn to read books that are not set up so quickly.

When we think about our own reading, we recall that sometimes stories start out differently from what we'd expected; yet these are often some of the best books we've read. As is the case with *Flying Solo,* we need to get to know the characters and become familiar with other aspects of the story first. We know that the decisions the author has made about the beginning of the story are deliberate. At the beginning of a book, readers begin to piece together information that will help them understand the rest of the story. As experienced readers, we know that there will be parts of a book that don't move as quickly as others. But we know how to get engaged in a book and how to stick with one once we have picked it. We have also learned that sometimes parts that seem unimportant or slow moving can be critical to the story. We love the beginning of books. We love to figure out how the pieces will fit together and where the author is going with the story. From the start, we come up with questions, predictions, and inferences, and we become fascinated as the story unfolds. Our students don't necessarily have the experience to know how to do these things. We need to support them in their reading until they can sustain interest and understanding on their own.

There are several things we could have done to support the sixth-grade readers in our earlier example. At first, we thought that maybe *Flying Solo* wasn't the right choice for them. But because they were truly interested in the book, we came to realize that they just needed a bit of support. Their suggestions that they skip the first twenty-five pages or that we read the first twenty-five pages to them helped us to see that their enthusiasm for the book was still strong. We knew that if we could help these students

Class Chart Brainstormed by Fourth Graders

When do you know you are hooked on a book?

- Time goes really fast.
- Can't stop reading.
- Can't put the book down.
- Relaxed—you have a good feeling.
- You are doing a lot of thinking without knowing it.
- You *have* to know what happens next.
- You can see and feel everything that's going on—like you're there.
- You want to buy the book.
- It gets exciting.
- You are trying to figure something out.
- You want to read it again.
- You keep asking yourself questions.

How do you read differently when you are not hooked? (Can be at the beginning of the book or in the middle of the book.)

- Hope for exciting times/hope that it gets better.
- Work hard to pay attention so you don't think of anything else.
- More predicting—makes you want to keep reading.
- Motivate yourself.
- Read it like it's a hard book (because it is not interesting).
- Remind yourself that a good part is probably coming.
- Trust other people who have read it.

get to page 26, they would probably be committed to reading the rest of the book. We also knew that experiencing a powerful book that unfolds slowly could help them grow as readers. Instead of having them choose another book, we had to find a way to support these students through those first pages *and* give them skills that would help them with similar books that they would read in the future. We didn't want to help them read just this book. After all, imagine how many great books our students would miss if they expect to be hooked on the first page of every one.

The first step in helping our students get through the beginning pages of many stories is to help them realize that all readers face this challenge. We sometimes ask students to interview adult family members and friends about books that took them several pages to get into. Then we have the children share what they have learned. Knowing that adult readers go through the same challenges in their reading often helps our students understand the importance of overcoming these challenges.

We also have students find books that they have read in the past—picture books and novels, books read independently, and books that were read aloud to them. We ask them to skim the books to see if they can remember when and where they became "hooked" on the book. Was it on the first page? Was it later? Then we ask the group what they could do to get through the beginning part of the new book.

During a similar discussion in a fourth-grade class, Chris reminded us that readers can become *un*hooked at different times in the book. He and his classmates remembered several places where a book they were reading moved a bit more slowly once they were already hooked. We talked as a class about how and why we'd keep reading when we aren't hooked, and wrote down our ideas. We then posted our list in the room as a reference for future reading.

As adults, we can trust that a book will be worth the energy it takes to read through confusing or less engaging sections because of our past experiences with books. We were talking with Cris Tovani about a book we are planning to read, *The Poisonwood Bible* by Barbara Kingsolver. The book has been recommended highly by friends whose opinions we trust. We've heard that it is a great book "if you can get through the first seventy-five pages." We have all read books that started slowly, but hooked us once we got to a certain point in the story. We know there is this magical moment when readers become so engaged that they no longer think of abandoning the book.

For children who have only recently started to read novels or who are encountering a challenging nonfiction genre for the first time, this need for

> **Books That Offer Quick Engagement**
>
> When we know that certain students have difficulty with books that do not hook them on the first page or two, we need to have books available for them that *do* get them involved quickly until they have developed strategies for reading books that develop more slowly. Here are some of our favorite books that get readers hooked from the very start:
>
> *The Watsons Go to Birmingham—1963* by Christopher Paul Curtis
> *Fig Pudding* by Ralph Fletcher
> *Joey Pigza Swallowed the Key* by Jack Gantos
> *Mick Harte Was Here* by Barbara Park
> A Series of Unfortunate Events series by Lemony Snicket
> *Wringer* by Jerry Spinelli

perseverance is difficult to explain. We need to think about ways to teach our students how to get through slow or confusing parts of a book. When we talk to adults about books like *The Poisonwood Bible,* many will say things like, "I am going to read that one when I have a long stretch of time for reading, so I can get into it." As adult readers, we know that with a book like *The Poisonwood Bible,* we won't ever get through those first seventy-five pages if we set aside only ten to fifteen minutes to read each day. We might be able to get through a Danielle Steele book with fifteen minutes each day, but books like *The Poisonwood Bible* require a different approach.

Supporting Older Readers

When we first started working with older readers, we were tempted to support them in the same ways we supported younger students years ago when we both taught first grade. As primary teachers we selected the children's books, introduced them to the books before reading, and guided them throughout the reading of the text. We knew the importance of matching kids with books, introducing the book, and guiding them at the early stages of learning how to read. Because we provided constant support, our students didn't always learn how to help themselves. They continued to be dependent on us well past the early stages of reading.

We worry when we see scripted book introductions that are so detailed they take all the thinking out of reading. Although an introduction provides a scaffold for the book students are currently reading, it doesn't give them what they need to start a book on their own. And we worry when teachers assess to see if students use the scripted introduction in their understanding of the book. By providing too much information before children read a book, we deprive them of opportunities to discover text elements as they unfold. With too much assistance, students come to think that good readers never get stuck and never get confused. They never know the joy of putting the pieces of a story together. Instead, they expect someone else (author or teacher) to do it for them. They begin to think that if they do get stuck or confused, it is up to a teacher or an adult to help them. We need to teach students the skills to use when they start a new book, get stuck, or don't have sufficient background knowledge. Although upper-elementary-grade students can read the words, they may not be able to understand the texts they are reading.

In her book *I Read It, but I Don't Get It,* Cris Tovani (2000) cautions us about our students who are "word callers." She writes, "Word callers have mastered decoding and, as a bonus, also choose to read. However, they don't understand that reading involves thinking. They go through the motions of reading but assume all they have to do is pronounce words. When they don't understand or remember what they have read, they quit. Word callers are fairly good students but often don't do well with tasks that require them to use the words they read to think on their own. These readers feel powerless because the only strategy they have for gaining meaning is sounding out words" (p. 15).

As we began to work with older readers we realized that children are ready to develop more sophisticated strategies on their own, but they need continuous instruction and support to become successful. We know that instead of sending children to the blue basket to find a book at their level, we can help them think about their own reading, learn about authors, understand their own strengths and challenges, and interact within a larger community of readers. Instead of introducing a new book to a child ourselves, we can teach him or her to preview the book, read reviews, and talk to friends before starting it.

Deep Reading

> One time I was waiting for my mom to get ready to go somewhere. So I read *Flying Solo* while I waited. I was reading so hard, when it was time to go, my mom almost left without me!
>
> Karynn

Several years ago, we both read *Tuesdays with Morrie* by Mitch Albom. Although the book is short and the words are simple, it was a very intense read with layers of meaning. If a readability analysis had been done on this book, we imagine it would have been rated "too easy" for the millions of Americans who read it. But *Tuesdays with Morrie* is not an easy book. The characters are complex and the message is profound. It is not a book we chose to read in one sitting because it took us to deeper levels of thought and response.

No matter which grades we have taught, we have found that children feel pressured to read longer, fatter books with smaller type and more challenging words. Their perspective is that longer is harder, and harder is better. When they talk about their goals in reading, they tend to imply that they believe that reading thick books quickly is the sign of a successful reader. As a result, we focus on helping upper elementary students (and their parents) recognize that reading deeply and understanding the complexities of a text are the real signs of a successful reader.

We look for books that support older readers in their understanding—books that seem easy at first glance but require deep thinking. If we always push students toward books that are longer and harder, they can never take the time to be thoughtful. They will be too busy "getting through" the books.

We talk about *Tuesdays with Morrie* with our students to make this point through our own experience as readers. We tell them that it is one of the most challenging books we have ever read, and yet the text looks *really easy*. We show them the words, the number of pages, and the size of the book. Yet this is not a "quick book," one that we could read in a day. We tell them that what made the book right for us was not the size of the words or the thickness of the book, but the thinking we did as we were reading. Then we often introduce several books in the classroom library that are short, but require deep thinking. We invite our students to read them during independent reading time. A lesson like this often validates books that are not lengthy and reminds kids that reading is about thinking.

Students learn that deep reading involves more than just sticking with a book. It means reading the text with the same enthusiasm during the hard parts as during the easy parts. We want our students to spend much of their reading time on books that are comfortable for them; but, in order to grow as readers, they need to stretch a bit. We also deliberately choose short texts with the potential for deep, thoughtful reading and conversation. Books like *Through My Eyes* by Ruby Bridges allow our students to understand the events depicted in the book but also help them understand what life might have been like for Ruby and her family. There are layers upon layers of insight to uncover in the text; uncovering them gives students a much deeper understanding.

Skills, Strategies, and Behaviors for Upper Elementary Readers

Our teaching is driven by the challenges that our upper elementary readers will encounter. We need to teach students that a new genre with unusual conventions is worth the energy it takes them to read, reread, and read again until they gain understanding. There are all kinds of ways to help students build these interests and skills. As Lucy Calkins (2000) writes, "In the teaching of reading, there are a handful of goals we need to work toward with decisiveness and firm clarity, so that we can accomplish them and move on to other goals" (p. 339). When we identify the handful of skills that are important for understanding increasingly complex texts, we can better think about the implications for instruction.

The following is a list of skills, strategies, and behaviors that we spend much of our time teaching to students in grades 3–6:

- Sustaining interest and understanding throughout a challenging text.
- Choosing books that match individual needs.
- Keeping track of characters.
- Using skills and strategies to get through the hardest sections of a text.
- Having the skills to get through text that is not interesting.
- Understanding complex meaning.
- Trusting that texts that aren't immediately engaging might have value.
- Reading a variety of texts with a repertoire of tools for working through different text conventions, formats, and features.
- Changing thinking while reading to revise predictions and clarify understanding.
- Having conversations in a community of readers with an increasing level of sophistication about different types of texts and reading experiences.
- Reflecting on thinking and monitoring strategies and behaviors.
- Knowing yourself as a reader.
- Using strategies flexibly for different kinds of text.

Readers in the upper elementary grades often struggle, for example, with book choice. How many times have they wandered in front of the book-cases and baskets of books looking for the next book to read? Do they know how the classroom library is set up, and do they know how to use it to their advantage? Can they transfer those skills to school libraries, public libraries, bookstores, and on-line bookstores? Do they have conversations with other readers about the books they are reading? Whom do they rely on for good book recommendations? Do they know other readers in the classroom well enough to make those recommendations? There are many classroom deci-sions we can make that will support our students' book choices, but we can only make good decisions when we know these readers well through conver-sations and observations.

Older readers need to develop certain behaviors, such as sustaining comprehension through a long text. We might have some insight from an assessment instrument that certain of our students are struggling in this area. But until we talk with them about their reading and watch over their shoul-der as they read, we might not know where and how comprehension breaks down for them. We need the information we gather in observations and con-versations to bring clarity and purpose to our planning and instruction. Teaching is a balance of knowing what our students need to learn and look-ing at each child as an individual learner.

We want our teaching to take older elementary readers to higher levels of literacy. To do this, we consider everything we do to be sure that we are teaching a more sophisticated perspective of reading and that we are passing the responsibility for understanding what they read on to our students. We plan how best to use space and time to foster a community of readers who have meaningful conversations about reading. We consider instructional experiences for our students that will help them understand that reading is thinking. We make sure that conversations in our reading workshop lead our students to deeper understanding. And we keep in mind that, like Courtney, our students are still learning to read.

Part One

CHAPTER 2

Organizing the Classroom Library

If I read a good book by a certain author, I don't have to take all day to find a good book by the same author.
       Shea

I use the Cleary section a lot more than others because I try to read every Henry Huggins I can find.
       Casey

The dim, dusty room . . . the cozy chairs, the globes, and best of all, the wilderness of books in which Jo could wander where she liked, made the library a region of bliss to her.
       Louisa May Alcott, *Little Women*

The library near her home when Karen was growing up was a weekly escape. She would walk out her front door and begin her journey with a sense of adventure. She was one of four children in her family, so she treasured the rare occasion when she could set out on her own. The smell of the books met her when she walked in the door, and the feel of the all-important library card in her back pocket was her ticket to a world of wonder. Anything she would ever want was there. Karen was a novice artist who loved to sketch, so art books on drawing techniques fascinated her. For a time, she was hooked on Nancy Drew and checked out every new book in the series that appeared on the shelves. For hours she would sit and read the inside flaps of dust jackets for stories that somehow connected to her emerging self. And sometimes she would just wander from shelf to shelf, browsing for a book that would somehow reach out and choose her. Karen came to know every corner of the library because for at least one day a week it was her adventure.

Karen learned to choose books from the library that were right for her at the time. She considered her interests, experiences, and purpose for reading. At first she may have taken out books that were too difficult or, for lack of interest, sat unread on her stack until it was time for another visit to the library. But over time she became skilled at choosing books from the library that defined her as a reader.

Choosing Books

We know that the more children read, the better readers they become. But students may be spending time with books that are too difficult or that are not engaging. Our role as teachers is to make sure that the right books are in students' hands at all times. When we consider our own reading as adults, we realize that "just right" isn't about readability alone. "Just right" books for us are books that are interesting, books that we are in the mood for at the time, and books that make us think. As we talk about books with our students, we can't be the ones who always take responsibility for putting "just right" books in their hands. It is time for students to start matching themselves with books.

Our role is to teach them how to choose books that they can understand and that sustain their interest. If our students begin to make meaningful choices, they are often more committed to the book. The best way to teach our students to choose appropriate books is to organize the classroom library thoughtfully. Even just the setup of the library can teach students much about what it is to be a reader. We know that if we group books by author, and if we begin conversations about why people often read several books by the same author, our students will eventually begin to choose books by an author they love; and if we organize our nonfiction books by topic, students will be better equipped to choose a book that interests them.

Learning from Bookstores

A few years ago we became interested in the ways in which our favorite bookstores are organized. The goal of bookstores must be to get the right books in the hands of readers. Books need to be displayed in a way that supports shoppers in finding the right books. We thought of our own reading and the ways in which we choose books when we walk into a bookstore. When we asked friends how they choose books in their favorite bookstores, we realized that readers have very different ways to select books. Some go straight to the best-seller table when they enter a bookstore. Some find their favorite author or genre and then choose. Some select books by topic. Often readers look for books that friends have recommended. Good bookstores are set up to support all of these different readers.

We spent time doing some research on the displays in local bookstores. We visited Cover to Cover, our favorite children's bookstore, as well as a large store that is part of a popular chain of bookstores. We talked to the owners about the ways in which they set up books to market them to the right readers. After visiting several bookstores, we found that they often display books in the following ways:

- Books are organized by genre.
- Nonfiction books are organized by topic.
- Many titles are displayed face out.
- Rotating displays appear in each section.
- Staff Picks/Oprah Book Club Books/*New York Times* Bestseller List are featured.
- Many titles by the same author are organized within a genre.
- New books are displayed in the same area.
- Popular books are easy to reach.
- Books that face out are displayed between several titles arranged with the spine out.
- Some titles may be found in two or three different places in the bookstore (new book section, by author, by genre).

We discovered that the "endcaps" are critical in bookstores. These are the areas at the end of each set of shelves that highlight a particular author, genre, or topic. Although the author, genre, or topic for the endcap remains the same, the books displayed are changed often. For example, science fiction readers know exactly where to go in a bookstore to find good science fiction books. During a visit to the bookstore one week, they might find a new book by Orson Scott Card on the endcap. When the same reader returns a few weeks later, a book by a different science fiction author will be displayed on this same endcap.

Bookstore employees are careful to put popular titles next to not-so-well-known titles, hoping that if readers are reaching for a book they've heard about, they may notice the one next to it and take a look at that one too.

Some bookstores have an employee assigned to each area of the bookstore. A worker who loves romance novels, for example, might become the romance expert, keeping up on new romance novels as they are published, reading reviews, and setting up the displays of rotating titles in the romance section of the bookstore.

Our local public library system has adopted display techniques learned from bookstores. In an article in the *Columbus Dispatch* (2002) titled "Libraries Borrowing a Page from Bookstores," the reporter, Jane Hawes, noted that circulation has increased dramatically at the libraries where staff are placing more books face out, as well as organizing and highlighting books in different ways. Susan Studebaker, director of extension services for the library, said, "One of the things studies have shown is that a lot of people don't have a particular title in mind when they come to the library. They just want to browse. The Dewey Decimal System doesn't lend itself to browsing."

Both of us buy books from large Internet bookstores. It is always fascinating to see which books pop up on our computer screens when we visit the sites. For example, the last time Karen signed on to an on-line bookstore, she was greeted with a list of recommended books chosen specifically for her. These on-line stores base such recommendations on other books we have browsed or purchased, recommending books by authors we have purchased before, or books on a favorite topic. They seem to know us as readers almost better than we know ourselves.

Implications for the Classroom Library

What we've learned from bookstores is that although there is no one formula for setting up the classroom library, there are techniques we can use that might help the readers in our classrooms. We constantly have to consider the categories in which our books are organized to make sure that they support students' book choice and engagement.

Years ago, we started to organize part of our classroom library books into baskets with similar topics, titles, or authors. We were pleased with the inviting look that resulted, but we realized that not all of the baskets were serving a purpose. We also tried to organize the books based on reading level. While children were better able to find books they could read with this organization, we realized that a system based solely on reading level wasn't really helping our students become independent in their book choice: picking out books only from a certain leveled basket was not teaching them how to decide whether a book was "just right" or challenging.

We have learned that we must first decide what we want to teach our children about book choice before we organize the classroom library. We know,

---

Questions to Ask When Setting Up a Classroom Library at the Beginning of Each Year

- How can the classroom library support good book choice habits? How can it support children as they think about themselves as readers, find favorite authors, read for different purposes?
- Will the entire classroom library be located in one area of the room or will different sections be in different parts of the room?
- Will nonfiction be in a different area from fiction? How will this help children learn why they read different genres?
- What type of reading materials will students have access to during reading time? Will they be encouraged to read magazines, news articles, comic books, or poetry?
- How will I find space to display books face out?
- Which displays will be permanent? Which will include rotating titles?
- Will I use baskets to organize books with the same authors, topics, and genre?
- How will I highlight less popular books to make them appealing to students?
- How will I make room to highlight books throughout the year based on student need?

for example, that if we have baskets of books that are organized by author, our children will start to discuss authors, recommend books by various authors, and discover favorite authors.

Books in Baskets

> When I come to finish a book, I go back to the same basket and I can get the same kind of book that I had read before. If the last book I read was good, I would get the same series.
> Karynn

When we started to display some of our books in baskets, our main goal was for the books to attract students. With the books facing out in the baskets, they were easy for students to browse. We were also pleased to find that when children put books away, they usually put them in the correct place! Although having a well-organized classroom library is a nice perk, it was never the reason we made the choices about book arrangement that we did.

We also considered the grade and developmental level of the students we were teaching. When Franki taught third grade, she dedicated many baskets to series books, because third grade is often a time when children are just learning to manage longer texts and when they often become interested in a series. Now that Franki is teaching fourth grade, she still has baskets of series books, but the series that she's highlighted are different, and the author baskets are more prominent.

Labeling Baskets

We are often asked how we teach our students to put books away in the correct baskets. We have avoided putting stickers on books because we want the children to understand why the books are where they are. Instead, we often have picture prompts on our labels. For author baskets, we have found photographs of the authors to put next to the author's name on each basket. This gives children a visual clue and helps them become more familiar with the author. For series books, we may put a picture of the main character on the label. We have found that by labeling the baskets in this way, children understand the organization and learn that the library is organized in ways that support them as readers.

Students can find books in a certain series.

We have used baskets to organize library materials in a variety of ways over the years to support the readers in our classroom. Here are a few of them.

Favorite Authors

I know exactly where the Newbery books are or different authors I enjoyed from the past.

Mia

Often the basket label includes the name of the author as well as a picture and some information about the author so children can begin to think about authors who would interest them. When books are categorized by author, children often learn that if they like one book by an author, they might like another one by the same author. Although all the books in the library are not organized by authors and placed in baskets, children often start to realize how important authors are in their book choice. They begin to pay attention to authors' names and ask about other books by authors who are not represented in classroom baskets.

In one third-grade class, Beth and Kristin were talking informally about Alfred Slote, an author they had recently discovered in the school library. Because a portion of the classroom library was dedicated to author baskets, the girls had learned how to find authors they love and how to talk about books in new ways. Even though there was no Alfred Slote basket in the classroom, these students introduced us to an author they discovered in their own reading.

We make sure to highlight authors who write in a variety of genres or who write various types of books. For example, Jon Scieszka and Ralph Fletcher are two of our favorites because both authors write a variety of

Students begin to have favorite authors.

Some authors, such as Ralph Fletcher, write in a variety of genres.

books. Again, grouping books by author takes the focus off the reading level and places it on other reasons for choosing a book. It also invites readers to try a genre they would not normally try. Students who loved *The True Story of the Three Pigs* will realize that Jon Scieszka also writes the Time Warp Trio series. Someone who loved *Fig Pudding* may decide to try one of Ralph Fletcher's poetry books. In the same way, we also try to find authors who write books of varying difficulty. We put all of Barbara Park's books together, including the Junie B. Jones series, *Skinnybones,* and *Mick Harte Was Here.* We place the James Howe books, including the Pinky and Rex series and *Bunnicula,* in the same basket. These authors appeal to many readers, but their books are written at different levels of difficulty. By putting all of an author's books in the same basket, we can validate the author choices children make without focusing on the level of the text.

Nonfiction Books

We usually organize nonfiction books by topic. In her book *True Stories: Nonfiction Literacy in the Primary Classroom,* Christine Duthie (1996) writes about the importance of separating fiction from nonfiction in the classroom library. By doing this simple thing, we can help children begin to learn that they walk to the nonfiction area when they are looking for information about gorillas, for example, but they walk to the fiction section when they

Students can browse nonfiction books by topic.

are looking for a story by a favorite author. Duthie also talks about another effect of organizing nonfiction books by topic: she writes that "arranging books by topic within genres gives individual nonfiction titles added power: Four books on a single topic grouped together on the same shelf seem to gain significance . . . A child committed to a certain topic is more apt to read all the available books on that topic if they are housed side by side" (p. 12).

Although readers may have favorite nonfiction authors, most choose nonfiction based on a topic of interest. By organizing nonfiction by topic, children learn how to find information. Molly Foglietti puts all of the baskets with books about animals on the same shelf for her third-grade students; she realizes that children interested in dogs may also be interested in horses. This type of organization is a great scaffold for children's moving on to the school and public libraries.

Favorite Series

We usually put all of the books in a series in one basket. Series books provide a great support for students as they move through the upper elementary grades. In an interview with Scholastic, author R. L. Stine states, "It excites me when kids write and say, 'I've read thirty or forty of your books.' It means

Books may be organized by series.

that they have developed a reading habit. And they will go on to read all kinds of books." We also make sure to place all the Cam Jansen series books in one basket with the Young Cam Jansen series, an easier version, to support a variety of reading abilities.

New Books

New books have their own basket in our classroom library. Although there is always a "New Books" basket, the books in the basket change throughout the year. This basket holds books that we get through book orders, books that we buy at conferences and bookstores, or books that our students have been waiting for because they are familiar with the author or series. Just as bookstores highlight new books, so do our classroom libraries. If we have read a review of a book we are all eagerly awaiting, we'll display the review somewhere near the basket.

Books We Have Read Together

We also have a basket for books and articles the class has read together. This basket grows fuller as the year goes on. It encourages readers to revisit and reread favorite books throughout the year.

Kelly takes a new book basket to a comfortable place in the room to browse.

Class Picks

A basket that holds our class picks is one with rotating titles. This basket serves as a place where students can recommend books to the rest of the class. When they finish a book that they think their classmates would enjoy, they can put it in the basket to encourage others in the classroom to take a look at it. Some teachers place recommendation sheets near this basket in case students have a particular friend in mind who they think would enjoy the book. Other teachers have the recommending students fill out an index card, telling classmates a little about the book and describing the kinds of readers they think might enjoy it. It is also helpful when the person who adds the book to the basket is somehow identified so that those considering reading the book know whom to talk to about it.

Read-Aloud Connections

The books in our basket of read-aloud books also change throughout the year. As we finish reading a book aloud to the class, we change the contents of the basket. We include the book that was just read aloud, but we try to extend student interest in two ways. We add additional books in the series as well as unrelated titles by the same author. For example, after reading Avi's *Poppy* aloud, we put the other books in the series (*Poppy and Rye, Ragweed,* and *Ereth's Birthday*), as well as other books by Avi, such as *The Secret School,* into the basket. Students who want to read more about the characters they've just been introduced to could choose the other books in the Poppy series for independent reading. Students who liked the author but were in the mood for a different kind of story might choose another title by Avi.

Favorite Characters

It is fun to read several books about the same character. Like the series basket, the Favorite Characters basket encourages students to read more about the same characters. As Richard Allington (2000) notes, "After a couple of books, the central character becomes familiar, predictable. It is easier to predict how DW will respond after having read several Arthur books, which means that you have read a lot about DW and her brother" (p. 64). Many of the Favorite Characters titles could also fit in the series book category, but the main character is more important than in other series. For example, in the Anastasia series by Lois Lowry, if a student likes the character of Anastasia he or she may want to read more about her, so we might include *Anastasia Krupnik, Anastasia at Your Service,* and *Anastasia on Her Own.*

Topic Sets

We also have baskets that include a variety of books on a specific topic that is usually interesting to upper elementary students. Each basket includes books in a wide variety of genres related to the topic. For exam-

---

Some Favorite Character Baskets

Character	Author
Poppy	Avi
Fudge	Judy Blume
Amber Brown	Paula Danziger
Joey Pigza	Jack Gantos
Judy Moody	Megan McDonald

A Sports Basket

These books, which represent many genres, may be placed in a single basket labeled "Sports."

Title	Author	Genre
Sports Pages	Arnold Adoff	Poetry
Home Run	Robert Burleigh	Picture book
Get Ready to Play Tee Ball	Jan Cheripko	Nonfiction
Soccer Halfback	Matt Christopher	Fiction (novel)
Center Court Sting	Matt Christopher	Fiction (novel)
Magic on Ice	Patty Cranston	Nonfiction
Macmillan Book of Baseball Stories	Terry Eagan, Stan Friedman, and Mike Levine	Short stories
For the Love of the Game: Michael Jordan and Me	Eloise Greenfield	Poetry/picture book
The Young Soccer Player	Gary Lineker	Nonfiction
Baseball Saved Us	Ken Mochizuki	Historical fiction
Dirt on Their Skirts: The Story of Young Women Who Won the World Championship	Dorreen Rappaport and Lyndall Callan	Nonfiction picture book

In addition, various laminated sports articles from *Sports Illustrated for Kids,* local newspapers, and issues of *Time for Kids* can go in the sports basket.

ple, the Dinosaur basket might include poetry books about dinosaurs, picture books about dinosaurs, and nonfiction books and articles related to dinosaurs.

Books Written in Letter or Journal Form

Sometimes we choose books because of the format in which they are written. Baskets can support this type of book choice. A basket of books written in letter or journal form, for example, might include books like *Dear Mr. Henshaw* by Beverly Cleary, *P.S. Longer Letter Later* by Paula Danziger and Ann M. Martin, *Amelia's Notebook* by Marissa Moss, and *Spider Boy* by Ralph Fletcher.

If You Liked————, You Might Like . . .

Rotating baskets can also be used to expand the idea of the Read-Aloud basket. Several "If you liked . . ." baskets can be in use at any one time. Such baskets are often suggested by popular books in the classroom—books that several children seem to enjoy. The idea is to help children choose a book when they are in the mood for something similar to one they've previously read. The books can be related by topic, genre, or author. For example, the basket labeled with "If you liked *Harry Potter and the Sorcerer's Stone*, you might also like . . ." would include fantasy stories like *Mrs. Frisby and the Rats of NIMH* by Robert C. O'Brien and *A Wrinkle in Time* by Madeline L'Engle. For students who enjoyed the picture book biography *Satchel Paige* by Lesa Cline-Ransome and James Ransome, other books about baseball might be placed in the basket (such as *Home Run* by Robert Burleigh), or the basket might include more biographies such as *Touching the Sky: The Flying Adventures of Wilbur and Orville Wright* by Louise Borden and *Pioneer Girl: The Story of Laura Ingalls Wilder* by William Anderson.

Award-Winning Books

We want our students to know about awards that are given to various books for their quality each year. We have a basket of award-winning books available to students throughout the year. Most of the books in this basket have won the Newbery Award. Others have been awarded the National Book Award for Children. Coretta Scott King Award winners (given to a distinguished African American author or illustrator) and Christopher Award winners (books that affirm the highest value of the human spirit) may also be included in this basket.

Newspaper and Magazine Articles

Newspapers and magazine articles may be laminated on tag board and placed in a basket organized by topic. We might have baskets of sports articles, bas-

kets of articles about current topics of interest, baskets of articles dealing with local issues, and baskets of articles from favorite children's magazines, such as *National Geographic Explorer, Time for Kids,* and *American Girl.* One student suggested that we keep single copies of all issues of *Time for Kids* in clear plastic sleeves organized in a binder.

Read with a Friend

The "Read with a Friend" basket or shelf holds at least two copies of various books that students may want to read together. This is where children go if they would like to read and discuss a book with a friend. This basket or shelf features a variety of authors, genres, and topics. Pairs of students can browse through this collection when they are in the mood to read a book that a friend is also reading. This collection lets our students know how important we think it is to read and talk with friends about reading, and it encourages informal book chat.

Keeping Baskets Flexible

At the start of the year, we leave some baskets unlabeled and empty. We will fill them when we get to know our students better. That way, if Gail Carson Levine turns out to be a popular author and we hadn't originally created a basket of Levine books, we can do so. In addition, several baskets hold rotating titles, such as the new books basket. A teacher we met in El Paso, Texas, had a great suggestion for the rotating baskets. She told us that teachers in her school use Velcro to attach the labels to these baskets so that they can be changed easily and quickly as classroom needs and interests change.

Each year, we worry about baskets that hold only a few titles. For example, when we only have two books by a certain author, we wonder whether it is worth an entire basket. But then we remind ourselves that our arrangement of books is really intended to teach children to make good choices and learn about being readers, so having many books in each basket is not a critical issue. It doesn't matter whether we have two books or fifteen books in the Matt Christopher author basket. What is important is that we have set up a way for children to realize that if they liked one book by Matt Christopher, they might want to read another.

School and public libraries can extend and support the reading our children do in the classroom. When Joey was hooked on books by Louis Sachar, he quickly read through the four that we had in our classroom basket. But there were several more books by this author in our school library and in our public library. The important thing that Joey learned in class was that he liked Louis Sachar and wanted to read more books written by him. He also knew when he visited the library how to look for a book that would be right for him. We can help our students make that connection to resources outside of the classroom by helping them use what they have learned about themselves as readers in the classroom.

Some teachers have multiple copies of lists of books in popular series or by a popular author, which they make available to students. Students who are hooked on a series or author can pick up a list and take it with them when they go to the school or public library so they can more easily find the books that are not available in the classroom.

Reading on the Internet

Baskets are not the only tools we use when organizing reading materials. Many of the materials available for our students to read are not placed in baskets. One area of growing interest is Internet reading. We are always looking for websites that would be good choices for our students' independent reading time. We try to find sites with lots of text and interesting pieces for our students to read. We book-

Some of Our Favorite Websites for Reading

Sites that extend the reading community for children:

www.gigglepoetry.com
www.kidsreads.com
www.spaghettibookclub.org
www.worldreading.org

Sites with author information and/or author biographies:

www.authorchats.com
www.dangutman.com
www.jeancraigheadgeorge.com
www.jerryspinelli.com
www.lemonysnicket.com
www.louiseborden.com
www.ralphfletcher.com
www.sharoncreech.com

Sites with great articles for children:

www.kidshealth.org/
www.nationalgeographic.com
www.sikids.com
www.stonesoup.com
www.timeforkids.com/
www.worldkidmag.com
www.zoobooks.com

Students read on-line during reading workshop.

Reorganizing the Nonfiction Library

Midyear, Franki realized her fourth-grade students were not reading much nonfiction. She met with the class and told them about her concern. They brainstormed a list of problems with the nonfiction books in the class library, made the following recommendations for reorganizing the books, and then worked together to reorganize the nonfiction books, using the list.

- Put the nonfiction section of books in a different place. It is in the back of the room and we never really see the books there.
- Make new labels. The labels are hard to read and they keep falling off.
- Organize the baskets so that topics that are similar will be together.
- Make a big "Nonfiction" sign to hang above the shelves so we remember to read nonfiction.
- Make sure the baskets aren't too full. Some of the baskets have too many books in them and they are hard to browse.
- Add more magazines to the nonfiction section.
- Have a separate recommendation basket for just nonfiction books.
- When someone reads a good nonfiction book, they should put a sticky note on the front cover with a note about why they liked it.
- Highlight some books on display racks, like a "Book of the Month."

mark these websites on the student computers and make them accessible to students during independent reading time. Hanging near the computers are color printouts of the home page of each website that we recommend. Students can look at these to see if a site interests them. During reading time, students can choose to read on the Internet, if they wish to go to one of these sites.

Many children also find great websites at home that we can add to our classroom list. For example, during Ohio's bicentennial year, we included the Ohio Bicentennial Celebration website, which provided interesting nonfiction reading related to students' social studies units.

Monitoring the Classroom Library

Throughout the year, we watch how children choose and talk about books. We constantly ask ourselves if the library organization is working. When we see that one area of the library is not working, we try to find ways to make it more engaging and purposeful,

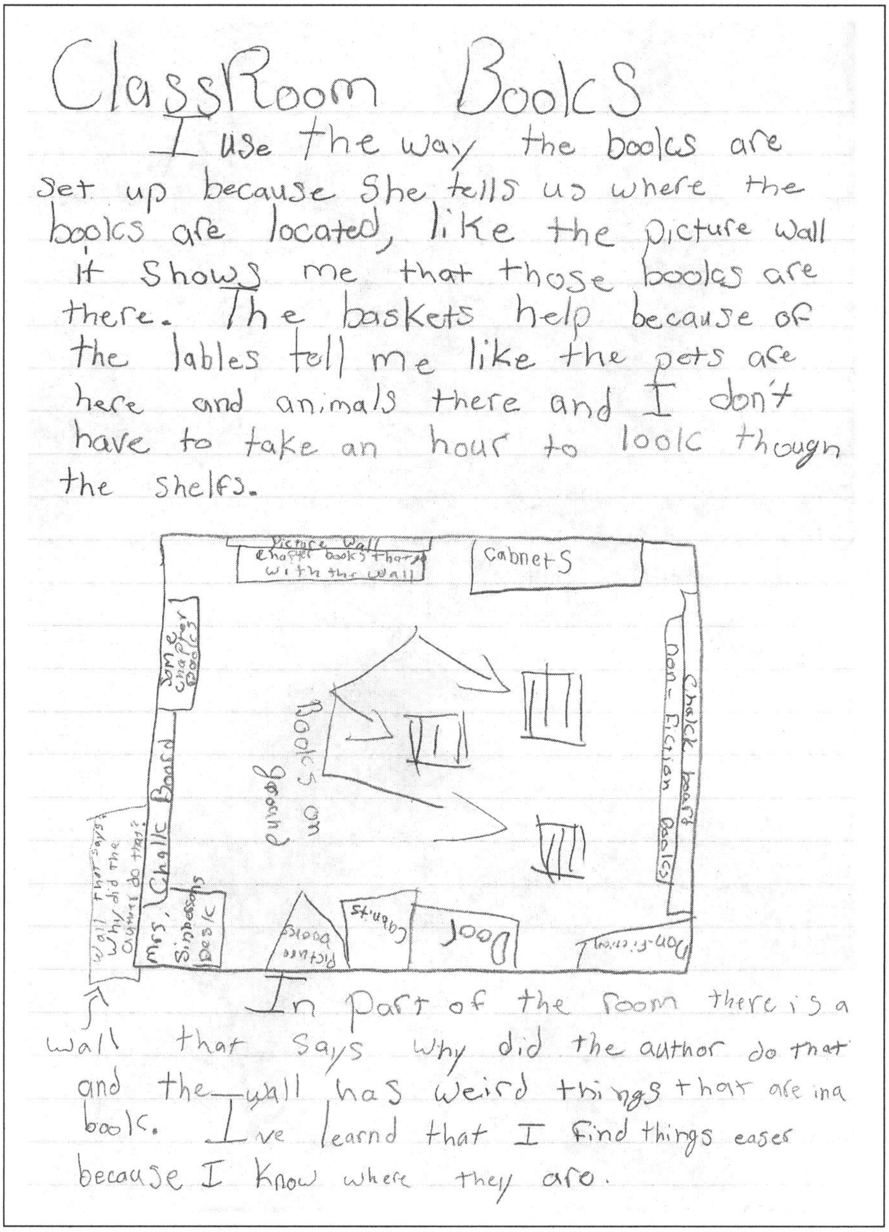

Figure 2.1 Leah's thoughts on the classroom from her reader's notebook.

ClassRoom Books

I use the way the books are set up because She tells us where the books are located, like the picture wall it shows me that those books are there. The baskets help because of the lables tell me like the pets are here and animals there and I don't have to take an hour to loolc though the shelfs.

[Handwritten classroom map with labels: Picture Wall, chapter books that go with the wall; Cabnets; some chapter books; Books on ground; Chalck board Non-Fiction Books; Wall that says why did the Author do that; Mrs. Simpsons desk; Pictures Books; Stunts; Door Cabnets; Non-fiction]

In Part of the room there is a wall that says why did the author do that and the wall has weird things that are in a books. I've learnd that I find things eases because I know where they aro.

or we reorganize the section based on our observations. When we taught third grade, we had a basket of books by Laura Ingalls Wilder that went untouched for a couple of months. After a few book talks with the students, we realized that this class was probably not going to develop an interest in these books. But they were hooked on the new Judy Moody books, which did not have their own basket. So we shelved the Laura Ingalls Wilder books with their spines out on a shelf (with students able to view titles only) and highlighted the Judy Moody books in a basket.

Our libraries are not completely organized into baskets. We use a variety of shelves, files, and other containers to organize the remainder of the library. Some of our books are arranged on shelves with their spine out. If all of our books are organized into baskets by topic, author, genre, or series, students will miss the fun of browsing. We want our students to enjoy the classroom library *and* to learn about ways to choose a book. We all are delighted when we come across a book that we've never heard of—one that looks great—and we end up loving it! Although most readers' book selection does not happen that way, we want children to be able to browse books in ways that allow such discovery.

Organizing the classroom library is always the most difficult and time-consuming part of preparing our classroom, and the organizing continues throughout the year. But it can make all the difference in the reading lives of our students. We want our students to consider the classroom library as an adventure in their lives as readers. The classroom library sets the boundaries and promotes endless possibilities for the reading community in our classroom, as Leah's musings on her classroom library suggest (see Figure 2.1).

CHAPTER 3

Preparing for Thoughtful Instruction

Our room is kind of surrounded by bookshelves. Pick your space in the middle of the room and whenever you need a book walk to the edge, find the right basket and get your book. It feels like a base of operations. You can use that base for anything you want.

Peter

Every fall, we return to school with plans for setting up our classrooms. In our heads, we've pictured what we might do with all the furniture, how our library could be organized, and where our meeting space will be. Every year we want to design the best space to support and extend our students' learning.

Karen remembers the year she worked for weeks to create the perfect classroom arrangement. Books were arranged to be accessible throughout the classroom, student desks were clustered in tables, a comfortable reading space took up one corner of the classroom, a table was set up as the science center, and a welcome mat was placed just inside the classroom door. Bulletin board space was planned so that each child had a place to post pictures, articles, and personal artifacts. Every inch of the classroom was designed to be inviting and engaging.

The week school was to begin, Karen walked into her classroom to find four brand-new computers and a computer table sitting in the middle of the room. She had to quickly rethink her classroom arrangement and still maintain the climate and purpose of her thoughtfully planned environment.

Setting up a daily schedule, organizing materials, designing bulletin boards, and creating a floor plan for the room at the beginning of the year are always challenging. Although we are committed to literacy instruction, we are also committed to the other areas of the curriculum. We know that we need to make the classroom library accessible and inviting for our students, but we also want the math and science materials to be accessible and appealing. We know that we need big blocks of time to teach reading, but we cannot sacrifice math, science, or social studies instruction in order for that to happen. When setting up the classroom and the daily schedule, we think about priorities. What are the things that we won't compromise? What do we consider the most important things? What are the implications for scheduling and room design?

Making the Most of Our Space

> I think it is good to have the option to read in different places because if you are someone who likes to read in a comfortable place or alone, you can choose the beanbag or your desk. Some other people might like to read together or in the same spot.
> Ben

The room has comfortable places for independent reading.

I think it is better to have a big space in the room because everybody can spread out and have their own thinking room. Like somebody might be moving their lips in the crunch space and you look over just a little bit and they mess up your thinking.

Blair

No matter how large our classroom is, it seems there is never enough space to do exactly what we envision. We have come to learn that in order to stay sane as we plan classroom setup, we need to set priorities first.

For example, we used to walk into a room and immediately set up the student desks first. Then we worked around them to find enough space for the rest of the areas that we needed. We have since realized that if we start with the learning spaces that are most important to us, we'll always find space for the desks. We are no longer worried that students at every desk be able to see the screen or front board, because we know that most of our whole-class lessons will happen with the children in the meeting area rather than at their seats. The way we set up the classroom gives our students a clear message about the culture of the classroom, the kind of work they will do, and the expectations we have for them.

When we plan our rooms each year, we have the following priorities:

- The classroom library needs to be organized in a way that makes sense for the children.
- There should be room for a meeting space large enough for the entire class, and this space must include an easel, an overhead, and individual tools such as clipboards and dry-erase boards.

A large space allows for whole-class lessons and conversation.

- There must be prominent space for other subject areas—math supplies, science, materials, maps.
- There should be comfortable spaces around the room for various size groups to meet, work on projects, talk, and read quietly.

These are the four priorities that we can't live without. Other features are less critical; we have even learned to live without a teacher desk if space doesn't permit. Of course, there are always parts of the classroom over which we have little control. Computers have to be placed where the data ports are installed. If the classroom has a television, it may be mounted to the wall and can't be moved. Screens and maps may be bolted in place. But by having only four priorities, we can still set up the room in a way that makes sense for our students and for us.

Once our floor plan is complete, we design the wall space. Our aim is to get students thinking about book choice. Wall displays will generate discussions that will last throughout the school year.

Using Wall Space

Whatever is on the walls at the start of the year will be the children's first impression of the year they will spend together. Much of the meaningful wall décor will come later. In the days and weeks to come, children will create charts, projects, and displays. It is tempting to leave the walls bare at the start of the year, because we know they will fill up quickly once the children arrive. But instead, at the beginning of the year we want to use this space to help students see what we value.

Stools provide a comfortable spot for small-group work.

Because we want our students to think critically in all areas of the curriculum, we try to balance the way we use our wall space. Some displays that we have used in the past include the following.

Ways into Books

To begin conversations about book choice, we've used one wall for series posters. We chose eight to ten series that we thought would be popular with beginning fourth graders. We made a poster for each that was headed "You might like this series if you . . ." During the first several weeks of school, students began talking about those series they enjoyed the most. One day, we asked students to put their name on two sticky notes and place them on the two series posters that were most familiar to them—two series on the wall that they could tell other readers about. Then the children whose names were on each series got together and filled out the poster telling about the books. For example, for the Horrible Harry poster, the students wrote:

> **You might like the Horrible Harry series if you . . .**
> like surprises
> like to read about troublemakers
> like funny books
> like characters who do weird things
> like to read stories about school
> like to read about characters that are all different

Next to each completed poster, photographs of the students who filled in the chart were hung, with a note that said, "If you want to know more about this series, ask these readers." The wall served several purposes. First of all, it helped the students think about things they could count on in series books. The posters helped students realize that different readers like different books. It also served as a great message to kids about the importance of recommending books to each other—kids asking kids about other books they'd read.

Book Characters

We also like to have books and book characters displayed prominently around the room. We collect posters from conferences and bookstores that we can cut up and use early in the year. If we know we will be using picture books often and want to get kids thinking about picture book characters, we may post as many as fifty to a hundred characters from books in one spot of the room. Next to the characters, a sign would read, "How many of these characters do you know?" Or we may display favorite series book characters above the series book wall. These boards get students thinking

A group of students sits on the floor around the coffee table to read poetry.

about characters they like, and conversations will naturally begin around books they've read.

Poetry

Poetry is often the least utilized book collection early in the year. To get kids more interested in poetry, we try to enlarge a fun poem, such as "My Dog Ate My Homework" by Sara Holbrook. In her book, *Wham! It's a Poetry Jam,* Sara gives kids ways to play with the poem; we post those possibilities next to the poem. The students are invited to sing the poem to a familiar tune or chant it with a group of other students. A display like this often gets kids having fun with poetry early in the year.

Invitation into Books

We keep our eyes open for books with pages that can be used as wall displays. For example, Bruce MacMillan's book *Puniddles* uses photographs as clues for word riddles. We purchased an extra copy of the book to cut apart and display. The book sits under the display. Our board of word riddles gets kids talking and having fun with words. Another book that we like is *Kidbits* by Jenny Tesar. This book

Books with Pages to Display Throughout the Classroom

Title and Author	Feature
Girls' Book of Wisdom edited by Catherine Dee	Quotes for girls
Punnidles by Bruce MacMillan	Picture riddles to solve
Grapes of Math by Greg Tang	Challenging math problems
Kidbits by Jenny Tesar	Interesting graphs with visual appeal
Brain Waves Puzzle Book by Rick Walton	Variety of puzzles to solve
The Kid Who Invented the Popsicle by Don L. Wulffson	Stories behind everyday inventions

Graphs from *Kidbits* invite children to read the book.

contains great graphs for kids. We use an extra copy and hang interesting pages around the room with a sign that asks, "What surprises you about this information?" Again, this kind of display not only gives students a great invitation into the book and to graph reading, it is also a place where kids gather to read and discuss the information displayed.

Word Play

We want our students to see that words can be fun, so we're always on the lookout for great word games that can be enlarged as a classroom display. For example, the Cleveland Indians programs often have terrific crossword puzzles and other word games dealing specifically with baseball. There are also several word games in each issue of *American Girl* magazine. A series of books with titles such as *Games and Giggles Just for Girls* by Paul Meisel and Jeanette Ryan Wall give us great ideas for beginning-of-the-year wall displays. We want word games that will invite kids to gather, problem-solve, and laugh through their thinking about words. A display like this is often hung directly above a basket of books about word play.

We struggle with wall spaces in the room that don't lend themselves to being used as often because they are not in the normal flow of daily activity. For

Books That Invite Students to Think About Words

Agatha's Featherbed by Carmen Agra Deedy
Dog Food by Saxton Freymann and Joost Elffers
A Chocolate Moose for Dinner by Fred Gwynne
Antics by Cathi Hepworth
Bug Off! by Cathi Hepworth
Alphabet Riddles A–Z by Susan Joyce
There's a Frog in My Throat by Loreen Leedy
A Huge Hog Is a Big Pig: A Rhyming Word Game by Frances McCall and Patricia Keeler
Food Fight! by Carol Diggory Shields
And the Dish Ran Away with the Spoon by Janet Stevenson
The Dove Dove: Funny Homograph Riddles by Marvin Terban
Too Hot to Hoot: Funny Palindrome Riddles by Marvin Terban

those spaces, we try to find permanent things to hang that give kids messages about the learning that will occur. For example, we've used four postcards that we've framed and hung near the classroom door. Each postcard has on it a single word: "smile," "celebrate," "laugh," and "create." These postcards remind kids about the best ways to work together in the classroom. The small frames give the words more importance than had we just hung the postcards up on the wall. We've also found great postcards with quotations about learning, which we've framed and hung above the bookshelves. These displays will not be replaced during the year, and they'll continue to give kids great messages about learning.

Making the Most of Our Time

Explore Time

Explore Time, sometimes referred to as Discovery Time, is a session of student choice activities. Students may decide to read, write, build something, conduct an experiment, or participate in a variety of other learning experiences. Charles Rathbone (1993) writes, "Explore Time offers the students time to do all of these things. It also offers the students the time to practice making choices, to take responsibility and ownership of their learning" (p. 93). During this time, teachers may meet with individual or small groups of students as necessary. Since Explore Time is not structured, it is easy to pull a group of students over to work on a specific skill or strategy. It expands our opportunities to meet with small groups or individual students and work on specific reading skills and strategies. In this way it extends the reading time in the classroom.

We also determine which experiences we need to make time for in the school day. Then, when the school's master schedule is complete, we work within the parameters to meet the priorities we have set. Some years, we're able to set aside a two-hour block for reading time. In other years, we've had to break reading time into shorter sessions scattered throughout the day because of the ways related arts, lunch, and recess are allocated in the school's master schedule. The schedule for the students' day may not be ideal because of the compromises we have to make as part of the master schedule. But we can still prioritize what we do in the classroom to support whole-group lessons, independent reading time, small-group instruction, thoughtful conversations, mini-lessons, and read-aloud time each day. We always make time for the following:

- Daily independent reading, as well as talk before or after independent reading. This is the time when small groups are pulled together for instruction. (30–45 minutes)
- Read-aloud. (15–30 minutes)
- Daily mini-lessons. (10–15 minutes)
- Opportunities for conversations and writing related to books and reading. (10–20 minutes)

Here are examples of daily schedules that have worked for two different school years:

Sample A

8:55–9:20	Explore time
9:25–9:40	Class meeting
9:40–10:20	Writing workshop
10:20–11:20	Math
11:20–12:15	Science/social studies/health
12:15–1:00	Lunch and recess
1:00–1:30	Read-aloud
1:30–2:20	Reading workshop
2:20–2:35	Recess
2:40–3:30	Related arts
3:35	Dismissal

Sample B

8:55–9:40	Writing workshop
9:40–10:00	Class meeting
10:00–10:45	Related arts
10:45–11:45	Math
11:45–12:30	Lunch and recess
12:30–1:00	Read-aloud
1:00–1:45	Reading workshop
1:45–2:45	Science/social studies/health
2:45–3:00	Recess
3:00–3:30	Explore time

Our daily schedules are much more flexible than they appear. We know we have limited time in each school day, and we know there will be some days when the reading lesson will take more or less time than the schedule states. If setup or cleanup for a science experiment will be an issue, we rearrange the day to fit our needs. We respond to these changes easily because we know that our daily schedule is a flexible guide for the learning experiences in our classroom. It provides a framework for thinking about our day at school, but it can be changed in response to instructional needs.

Creating Routines for Conversations and Writing

> *I remember a time when someone said something and I did not agree. So I said, "Where in the book does it say that?" and they proved me wrong.*
> *Blair*

There are certain conversations, questions, and lessons that we want to build on throughout the school year. When we extend conversations in this way, students' understanding deepens.

We try to design our classroom space to nourish and challenge readers and writers. We set aside large chunks of time to immerse our students in reading and writing and to promote thoughtful conversations

Questions That We Ask Our Students to Think, Talk, and Write About Throughout the Year

The following questions are ones we use throughout the school year to deepen students' understanding and extend their thinking. These questions help our students name the things that they are doing so they become more aware of their own use of strategies.

Knowing yourself as a reader

What did you learn about yourself as a reader?
How have you changed as a reader?
How will this affect your independent reading?

Reading difficult text

Where did you get stuck? What did you do to help yourself?
What made that part/text difficult to understand?

Using evidence from the text to support your thinking

What in the text makes you think that?
How does this evidence help you understand the text more deeply?

Changing your thinking while reading

Where did you notice that your thinking had changed?
Why do you think that your thinking changed?
What in the book led to your change in thinking?

Rereading (reading again, reading differently)

When you reread, how did you read differently?
What did you notice when you reread that you didn't notice the first time?
How did rereading help you understand the text better?

The power of writing and talk

Did anything in your conversation today help you understand something about the text more deeply?
Did writing cause you to think about something you hadn't thought of before?

and rigorous learning. But, perhaps most important, early in the year we strive to establish routines that support students' growing independence as readers. Many of these routines include common questions and conversations around texts and the use of reading notebooks to extend the conversations in writing.

Reading Notebooks: Writing to Develop Thinking

I never knew I could still be learning how to read to become a better reader. I actually (sometimes) really want to use my reader's notebook because I really get good ideas and I want to keep them forever.

Karinn

Although we do not give written tests or use end-of-chapter comprehension questions, we do want a place for our students to record and reflect on their growth as readers. During a visit to Judy Davis's classroom at the Manhattan New School, we saw how powerful reading notebooks could be. We have used reading notebooks ever since and have revised them often to meet the goals we have for our students. These notebooks give us the information we need to plan whole-class activities as well as small-group and individual instruction. We refer to them continuously to analyze and assess student needs.

During the summer before we began using reading notebooks with students, we each started one of our own. We knew that having a model to show our students would be important, and we also knew that many mini-lessons could come from our own reflections as readers. We purchased fun spiral notebooks from a local stationery store and separated them into sections. We spent the summer filling these sections with thoughts and responses to our reading. Our notebooks continue to help us think of new ways to work with our students in the area of reading. By attending to our own reading reflections, we can better understand how our students think about their own reading. For example, Franki records what books she has read and checks her reading log from time to time to see if her reading is balanced by genre. She is interested to know whether she reads more fiction or nonfiction, more adult novels or more children's novels.

We currently divide the reading notebooks into five sections. These five sections support the reading behaviors that we want our students to practice. The notebook serves as a place for each child to capture his or her thinking and reading experiences throughout the school year.

Reading Log and Response

The "Reading Log and Response" section of the notebook is a place for students to keep track of books completed as well as those started and abandoned. This section is where they can write assigned and unassigned responses, as well as a place for them to record favorite lines of text, questions they have as they read, and thoughts for books read during independent reading. This section of the notebook is a great way for students to begin their reflective thinking about reading. We encourage them to look at this section to consider what they have been reading and to notice what genres they have not read as yet. By keeping track of their reading over long periods of time, students can see how they are changing as readers and can easily set goals for themselves. Over time they can see patterns in their reading.

Many students read with their notebooks nearby.

Students organize this part of the reading notebook in different ways depending on the purpose. At the beginning of one year, Franki asked her fourth-grade students to write information in their reading log each time they finished a book. (A form for this type of organization is provided in the appendix.) After a few weeks, Franki realized that her students were not consistently using the log and were forgetting to record their reading. So Franki changed the log to a daily record of their reading. At the end of each reading workshop, students complete their logs. They record the date, the name of the book, the author, and the pages they read that day. (See Figure 3.1.)

Figure 3.1 Jordan's reading log.

There is no one right way to keep a reading log. If you want students to begin reflecting on favorite authors, you might have them include the names of authors they have read in the log. If genre balance is important, you might want to have a column where students list the genre of each title. Have the log match your instructional goals, which in turn are based on student needs.

Books I Want to Read

The "Books I Want to Read" section of the reading notebook helps students look ahead in their reading. It helps them plan what they might read next and is a place for them to think about the books they want to read in the future. Here, students may make a list of books they may want to read, paste any book reviews they've cut out and want to keep, or include photos of book covers to support them in choosing

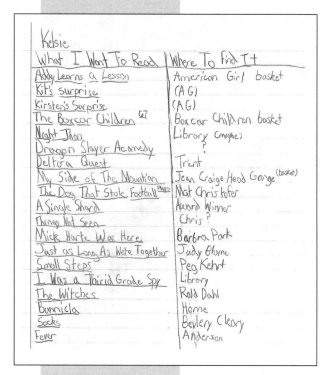

Figure 3.2 Kelsie keeps track of books she wants to read in her notebook.

Figure 3.3 Tessa decides to focus her response to *Wringer*. Each day she asks herself, "What would I do in Palmer's place?"

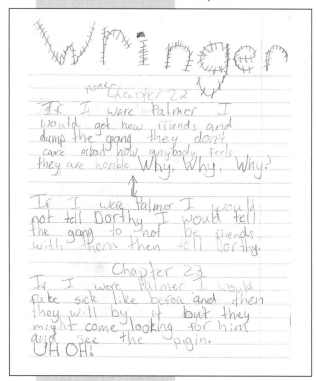

books. This section of the notebook helps them to think ahead in reading as well as pay attention to ways that their tastes are changing and expanding.

In our own reading notebooks, we keep lists as well as book reviews that we cut out of magazines. Franki even has a napkin taped in her notebook from a visit to a local bookstore. The napkin was the only thing she had to write on when she found several books to add to her list. A great resource for students is the website www.kidsreads.com, which has hundreds of book reviews and summaries.

By sharing entries in our reading notebook with students, they learn ways to think ahead in their reading. We also encourage them to note where they can find the book when they are ready to read it—in the classroom, in the school library, or perhaps a friend has it. (See Figure 3.2.)

Read-Aloud

The "Read-Aloud" section of the notebook is dedicated to whole-class read-aloud books. Children respond to each book in different ways, depending on the instructional focus. This section helps students keep track of their thinking and practice a strategy. Although informal, it can spark purposeful conversations and support a more thoughtful view of reading aloud. After finishing a read-aloud of *Wringer* by Jerry Spinelli with open responses, one class made a list in their notebooks of all the types of responses they had during the session. Their notes showed them how responses to the same text may vary and how writing can help develop one's thinking about a book. Later in the year, we might choose to focus on specific types of responses (as Tessa has done in Figure 3.3), but encouraging open-ended responses in the notebooks helps students develop their own thoughts around a book.

This section of the reading notebook also serves as a record of the books the class has read together. Following each read-aloud, students look back through the book and choose a page that they would like to keep in their reading notebooks. We then make a copy of that page for each student to paste into his or her reading notebook as a reminder of the read-aloud experience. Students can respond to the part of the book that they remember most vividly or the scene that meant the most to them.

Students also keep book preview information in this section. For example, before beginning the book *The Tiger Rising* by Kate DiCamillo, students previewed the book by studying the front cover, back cover, inside flap, and the first page and by thinking about what they already knew about the author. Then they wrote their thoughts about the book in this section of their reading notebook. Not only does this teach students previewing skills, it also gives them a place to track their thinking over the course of the book.

Me as a Reader

We also include a section in the reading notebook called "Me as a Reader." Here students write their thoughts about themselves as readers. Students reflect in this section at least once a week as part of a mini-lesson or whole-class conversation. They may reflect on a quote about reading, a book we've shared, a question posed to them, or something they noticed in their own reading. At certain times during the school year, we ask our students questions about their reading or have them reflect on their reading log. These reflections help them to define and redefine themselves as readers throughout the year. (See Figure 3.4.)

Strategies and Mini-Lessons

The fifth section of the notebook, "Strategies and Mini-Lessons," overlaps with the other areas of the notebook. We use it to keep track of specific lessons using primarily short text. For example, when we read a book and ask students to question the text, these questions are recorded in this section of the notebook. When students work through a newspaper article or if we model a particular strategy, the

---

Types of Responses in Reading Notebooks During the Reading of *Wringer*

Things that surprised me
Predictions
Things I wondered/questions
New things I figured out
Important things
Evidence for an interesting question I stuck with for a while:
    Is Beans a good friend?
    Would Palmer keep Nipper?
    Would I do what Palmer did?
    Will Beans find out about Nipper?
    Will Beans ever change?
    Does Henry want to be part of the group?
Summary of chapter
What would I do in the situation?

Books That Have Great Quotes to Write and Talk About from Our Histories as Readers

Life Is So Good by George Dawson and Richard Glaubman
Reading Magic: Why Reading Aloud to Our Children Will Change Their Lives Forever by Mem Fox
What the Dormouse Said by Amy Gash
Looking Back by Lois Lowry
How Reading Changed My Life by Anna Quindlen
For the Love of Books by Ronald Shwartz

Figure 3.4 Karýnn writes her first entry in the "Me as a Reader" section of her notebook.

Dear Mrs. Sibberson,

    I like to read in my own special way. Some time I have to be in the mood to read. I like to read nonfiction books. I really like to read more things that are like people that do things as people would do now.
    Sometimes I will sit on the floor and read, or some times in my seat. I really like to have someone read to me. At home I read books from the library, and books that my mom recamends to me that I like to read.

      I hope you like my letter,
        From,
        Karýnn

Casey and Jordan use their notebooks during a mini-lesson.

article and sticky notes that students use are placed in this section of the notebook. Students use this section of the notebook during whole-class, small-group, or individual conferences. Some of the lessons are not necessarily strategy based. When we realized that one group of fourth graders thought that all poetry rhymed, we had them pore over stacks of poetry books, jotting down things they noticed that they never knew about poetry. (See Figure 3.5.) This section can also capture much of the learning that is not connected to independent reading or read-aloud.

Because we have to grade our students, we are always tempted to grade the responses in the reading notebook. When we asked our students how they would feel about their notebooks being graded, they were candid with their responses. Andrew said, "If you graded our notebooks, every time you write you'd be so concerned whether your thinking was good enough." Glen told us, "If you graded our notebooks, we'd be more worried about getting an A than about our thinking." Although we sometimes give points or credit for keeping a reading log updated or for children's identifying places in their log where they have changed their thinking, we know that if we started to put a grade on the writing in their notebooks, the purpose of the notebooks would change. It would no longer be a safe place for students to develop and deepen their understanding of reading.

Figure 3.5 Mia discovers new things about poetry.

> **Poems**
>
> | Something new | Something old |
> |---|---|
> | Poems can be a Story | Poems don't need to rhyme |
> | Poems can tell about someone | Poems can be said happy or upsetting. |
> | Poems can be mysterys like "my drawer looks confused." | |
> | Poems about poems | Some poems can be songs |
> | Some poems can be VERY short. | Some poems can be true others can be fiction |
> | Some poems you have to read in a different passions. | Some poems can be shaped funny like this. |
> | Some poems look like this teacher— | |
> | hate | |
> | Alex | |
> | Some poems you have to read over and over again | |
> | made up words. | |

We have learned that writing in response to reading can no longer be the end product. When children are asked to talk about and write about their thinking about their reading, they often develop new ideas *because* of the writing and talk. We want our students to see the power of both writing and talk as a tool for thinking.

Our goal each year in setting up our classroom is to create an inviting environment that will engage learners. Even when we find four computers plunked down in the middle of the room the week before school begins, we know we will be fine if we always design and redesign based on what we value the most about teaching and learning.

CHAPTER 4

Slowing Down During the First Six Weeks

Confessions of a Reader

Almost spring
A spider
Stakes a claim
On a corner
Of the eight-foot window
In our living room.

Each morning
I admire
Taut guidelines
Carefully placed spokes.
Dancing gown threads,
Architecture unrivalled.

My mother
Would not tolerate
Such slovenly housekeeping.
She would get a broom
And knock down
This errant squatter's palace.

I do not.

I am waiting for Charlotte
To leave a message.
     Carol Wilcox

I've been reading harder books and finishing them not so fast. In second grade, I used to find another book I wanted to read and read my first one really fast. And now I have grown out of that habit.

Jordan

In these days of mandated standards and high-stakes testing, it is often difficult to remember our overall goals for our students. Of course it is important that they pass high-stakes tests and that they meet the educational standards set by our state and nation. However, we want more for our students than to merely pass tests. Like the reader in the poem above, we want our students to live joyfully literate lives. It is sometimes most difficult to remember this in September, when school begins. As teachers, we enter the school year knowing what our students are capable of and wanting to jump right in, teaching those skills that are necessary at their grade level. We worry that someone will think we are wasting time when we take the time to build a community and have conversations about books. We worry that our time should be spent teaching the skills and strategies that will be tested in the spring. But we believe that helping our students develop new attitudes and behaviors leads to new skills and strategies for understanding the texts they read.

We use the first few weeks of school to find out which skills and strategies students in our class already have, so that we can use classroom routines to build on these. In her book *What You Know by Heart: How to Develop Curriculum for Your Writing Workshop,* Katie Wood Ray (2002) says, "Filling a classroom up with possibilities for how this work might go is really at the heart of teaching writing" (p. 80). We believe that this is just as important in the teaching of reading. Our role as teachers is to fill up our classroom with the possibilities of being a reader. Doing so lets children find their own identity as readers—to discover their preferences as well as the strategies that work for them. The beginning of the year is the perfect time to validate the possibilities of the reading workshop that will be important throughout the school year.

Where Do We Begin?

Early in the school year there are so many things that we need to do and so many places we want to go. As Lucy Calkins writes in *The Art of Teaching Reading* (2000), "In September, the challenge is not deciding what to teach, but deciding what not to teach. The art of teaching reading is always about selection, but this is never more true than at the start of the year" (p. 342). The conversations we start in September will begin the conversations and learning we have throughout the year. We need to go slowly. We usually spend the first several days talking informally with students about their reading. These first conversations help us find out where our teaching must begin.

We used to rush to fit in our district assessment during the first few weeks of school. Our district requires us to administer the Developmental Reading Assessment (DRA) to each student before the end of November. The information we gain from this assessment is valuable. But the information we gain from informally interviewing our students about their reading is even more important at the start of the year. When we take the time to ask students questions about reading, we not only learn about our students, but we also teach our students what is important in our classroom. Many intermediate students still believe that reading is about "getting all of the words right." When we give a reading assessment like the DRA before we have had time to talk to our students individually, we reinforce that definition with our students. However, when we begin the year by chatting with our students about their likes and dislikes and struggles and strengths as readers, we teach them that reading is more than getting the words right and answering questions. We also teach them that we are interested in what they have to say and that we are fascinated by their lives as readers.

When we talked recently to a group of fourth-grade students about their lives as readers, we asked questions like "How do you choose books?" and "What do you do when you get to a word you don't know?" Here is what we learned:

- Many of the students were interested in "reading harder books—books that were long and had hard words in them."
- Students thought texts were hard when they couldn't say the words correctly.
- A very small number of students read and enjoyed poetry and nonfiction.
- Most students had few strategies for dealing with unfamiliar words.
- Students had never been asked these questions about themselves as readers.

As early readers, children measure their success as readers by their decoding skills. But as they move into the upper elementary grades, they need to understand their lives as readers. They are ready to begin thinking about the strategies, behaviors, and attitudes that shape their reading lives.

Beginning by Knowing Yourself as a Reader

I read differently now than I did fifteen years ago. I have moved from a passive to an active stance. I am acutely aware of my own reading process,

the questions and challenges I have for authors I read, the awareness I
have of moments of confusion and disorientation in the text, and the tools
I use to confront that confusion.
    Ellin Keene and Susan Zimmerman

So much of what we know about teaching reading we have learned through our own experiences as readers. Teaching reading in the upper elementary grades is a constant process of monitoring our own strategies with texts we enjoy and texts with which we struggle. As we learn more about our reading, we can use this knowledge to help our students. The challenge is to keep the talk natural and the connections unforced between our reading and the behaviors we want to see in our classrooms.

Richard Allington (2000) notes the gap between the ways adults talk about books and conversations in classrooms: "Imagine that you are talking with a friend. Imagine that you ask a known-answer question. You ask for the location of the nearest hardware store, even though you already know the answer. Your friend replies, correctly, and you give her a sticker and say, 'Good job, you've got your thinking cap on.' Would your friend be pleased with your reply and the sticker? Or confused, wondering whether you've gone mad? We do not quiz friends on the newspaper articles they've read. Nor the books they've read. However, we do discuss the articles and books. We engage in conversations about the text, typically focusing on ideas in the texts" (p. 88).

As readers, we anticipate our future reading and watch for books by our favorite authors. We are both waiting for the next book by Anna Quindlen to be released. We have heard her speak, read reviews of the upcoming book, and searched for it on the Internet. We share our anticipation with students so they recognize that we all have certain behaviors that support our reading. It is not just the strategies we use while we are reading that we want to share with our students. We want to show them the behaviors and attitudes that make us unique as readers as well as the ones that we share, the ones that bring us together as members of a wider reading community. Anna Quindlen (1998), in her book *How Reading Changed My Life*, writes, "Part of the great wonder of reading is that it has the ability to make human beings feel more connected to one another" (p. 39).

In our first whole-class lessons, we often take a few minutes to share our own experiences as readers in order to provoke informal talk about the ideas and concepts in books, as well as reading behaviors. We will continue these lessons about our experiences throughout the year. Just as we considered our own book shopping habits when we organized our classroom library, we do the same when we are planning how to teach a skill, strategy, or behavior to our students. When we read a book or magazine at home and have insights about our own reading that we think may someday help our students, we bring that book to school. There it sits on a shelf in the classroom, so that we'll have it when we see the need to use it with students.

For example, when Franki was reading *The Red Tent* by Anita Diamant she found herself constantly going back to the second page of the book, the page that introduces four of the main characters. For the first fifty pages of the book, Franki could not keep track of who was who in the story. She knew that in order to understand the rest of the book, she would need to clarify her understanding of the characters and their relationships. The second page supported her until she knew the characters well enough. Franki now keeps this book on her shelf because she knows that keeping track of characters in novels is a skill that many transitional readers struggle with as they become more independent.

When Franki finds that many of her students are moving into books with more characters and are having difficulty keeping track of them, she shares the strategy she used in *The Red Tent*. This likely will lead to talk about other strategies that readers can use to keep track of characters in books. Franki's experience with *The Red Tent* often becomes the beginning of a series of lessons on character development. By starting with her personal experience, Franki lets her students know that keeping track of characters can be a challenge for any reader and that they can develop strategies for making their way through books with complex character development. The focus of these lessons from our lives as readers is always to encourage our students to learn strategies that will help them when they read independently.

As we work with students and we recognize an opportunity to teach a behavior or skill, we share our saved texts with them. These are not books that we would read to children; they are usually adult books. Yet, we show these books to our students and use them to share what we noticed about our own reading.

We use not only our own stories, but also each other's stories and the stories of children we have known in our teaching. We keep stories of former students in our heads. We remember how hard it was for Christy to choose a

Franki's and Karen's List of Books to Share with Students

Franki's Books

Title and Author	Focus for Sharing
Wanderer by Sharon Creech	Linger longer with a story by reading favorite lines and passages that have been marked in the text.
Sister of My Heart by Chitra Banerjee Divakaruni	Shifting scenes, characters, and narrators between chapters.
Where the Heart Is by Billie Letts	Living with a story and its characters long after you have finished reading the book.
Crossing to Safety by Wallace Stegner	Rereading to notice new things about the story and understand it more clearly.
Anna Karenina by Leo Tolstoy	Has the skills to read it, but needs a longer stretch of time (like the summer) to read it.

Karen's Books

Title and Author	Focus for Sharing
Portrait in Sepia by Isabel Allende	Becoming familiar with a complex set of characters and the connections among them with a family tree.
Life Is So Good by George Dawson and Richard Glaubman	Understanding the time period in which a story takes place.
The Secret Life of Bees by Sue Monk Kidd	Using information presented by the author to go deeper into the story to uncover complex meanings and themes.
My Dream of You by Nuala O'Faolain	Noticing text features and reading without typical supports (quotation marks).
Empire Falls by Richard Russo	Recognizing a possible theme in the story and reading to sustain or revise thinking.

book after finishing *A Wrinkle in Time* by Madeleine L'Engle because she couldn't find one that was "even close to being as good as that!" Sharing Christy's story with our present students helps them learn about other readers' habits and behaviors. We can then help them decide whether they want to read a book of a totally different genre to avoid disappointment or whether they want to try another book by the same author. When we share other readers' stories, it reminds our students how important it is to talk to other readers. Sharing stories also lets our students know that others often struggle with the same kinds of things that they are struggling with. It also lets them know that even good readers sometimes get stuck. They begin to learn that good readers are not people who never get stuck, but people who know what to do when that happens.

We also share our professional reading with our students. We know that work-related reading is an important part of who we are as readers. Our children are fascinated that there are books written about how to teach students! They are also interested to see that our reading also affects what we do in the classroom.

Although Franki may share her experiences about the way she kept track of characters in *The Red Tent* with one class, she may find that another class would not need that lesson. Because our students and their needs can vary so much from year to year, our own reading experiences become a crucial guide for designing instruction.

Students Reflect on Their Reading Lives

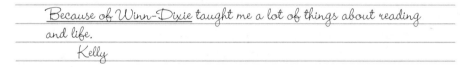

Because of Winn-Dixie taught me a lot of things about reading and life.

Kelly

Several weeks at the beginning of the school year are spent helping our students learn as much as they can about themselves as readers. Early in the year, when we ask students questions about their reading, their answers are usually somewhat shallow. Often we get blank stares, a quick comment like "I don't like to read" or a puzzled response like "I don't know. No one has ever asked me that before." We always worry when we get these responses that maybe this group of students won't be as thoughtful or as reflective as the previous classes we have had. Somehow, each September, we forget that it takes time and conversations to help students become reflective about their learning.

Because we know it is important for children to know themselves as readers, many of our lessons during the first few weeks of school invite the students to think about different aspects of their lives as readers. We start the year reading books about reading, such as *The Library* by Sarah Stewart. We also read them Ellen B. Senisi's *Reading Grows*. This picture book follows children through reading development, from their being read to as infants to their becoming proficient readers on their own. It is a simple book, but it gets students thinking about their growth as readers. They begin to use the "Me as a Reader" sections of their reading notebooks to respond to questions and quotes about reading. Their entries help us continue the conversations and thinking that we began with our informal reading interviews. (See Figure 4.1.) Here are some questions that we have found useful to get children thinking about their reading:

Which series books do you like? Why?
Is there a book from your childhood that you asked your parents to read over and over and over?
Which books do you remember from the years that you were just learning to read?
What was your favorite book when you were little?

We also send students home to do some research. They ask family members what they remember about the student as a reader. What were they like when they were toddlers? Which books did their parents remember reading over and over and over? (See Figure 4.2.) A form for such an interview is contained in the appendix.

After several conversations about their lives as readers, we ask each student to look through the entries in his or her reading notebook and write a piece that puts it all together. A form along the lines of the "Reflecting on Reading" page in the appendix may be used. The students celebrate growth and change as they reflect on who they are as readers. This experience not only helps students get to know themselves, it also lets them get to know their classmates. It is an important piece in building the reading community.

During these early weeks, one of the quotes that students respond to is from Mem Fox's book *Reading Magic* (2001): "Most of us think we know what reading is, and that's not surprising. After all,

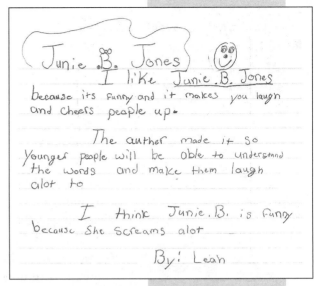

Figure 4.1 Leah thinks about a series that she enjoys.

Figure 4.2 Kelsey learns about her reading history by interviewing her family.

Easy Books to Help Redefine Reading

Grandpa's Teeth by Rod Clements
Click, Clack, Moo by Doreen Cronin
Bark, George by Jules Feiffer
Bamboozled by David Legge
Ring! Yo? by Chris Raschka
Don't Let the Pigeon Drive the Bus! by Mo Willems

we can read. But reading is tricky. Reading is complex" (p. 75). When we give this quote to students and ask them to read it and to write their definition of reading, the students are sometimes confused. They groan that this kind of thinking is "too hard." It is clear that they haven't thought much about what reading actually means to them, or that they have a very limited definition of reading. Most of the students write just one or two sentences, almost always mentioning "figuring out words" or "getting the words right" or "sounding it out." Only a few students mention understanding or meaning. Redefining reading is the next step for these students.

One good resource to help students redefine reading is the book *Bark, George* by Jules Feiffer. This is a hilarious picture book meant for very young children. With upper elementary readers the challenge is getting students to become interested in a book that clearly looks like a book written for preschool students. But the humor and the conversation about the book hooks them. In *Bark, George*, the text and the illustrations work together to tell the story. For a mini-lesson in September, Franki read the text aloud, one page at a time. After each page, she asked the students what they were thinking. Students shared their responses, predictions, changes in thinking, and inferences. (The surprise ending elicited the best responses.) Franki ended the lesson by asking the kids to remember all of the thinking that they did. Then she said, "Wow, if you did that much thinking in *this* book, imagine how much thinking you must be doing in the books you are reading during reading workshop." Instead of defining reading for the students, Franki hoped that this lesson would begin to make them curious about what readers do. Franki could have taught her students all about the habits of effective readers. Instead, she decided to help them gradually discover for themselves what readers do and to uncover their own lives as readers.

On the following day, Franki read *Click, Clack, Moo* by Doreen Cronin, another amusing picture book that engages readers. This time, she asked students to use the Strategies section of their reading notebooks to track their thinking. She read the book aloud and asked students to write down their thinking as she finished each page. Once in a while, they would stop and discuss the kinds of thinking they were doing. The students were amazed at how much thinking they were doing along the way. The last page of *Click, Clack, Moo* is critical to the story, but it contains only an illustration, no words. After finishing the reading, Franki turned again to the last page and asked, "Was this reading?" The children started talking all at once. Some were saying, "Yes!" Some were saying, "No!" Some were saying, "Yes and no." Some children were frustrated by the question. They argued that it couldn't be reading because there were no words. They argued that it had to be reading because without that final page, the story would be different. The conversation over that one page lasted twenty to thirty minutes, with Franki saying very little. The students' definitions of reading were beginning to change. They were developing a deeper understanding of what readers do. Finally Franki stopped the conversation and asked the students to go back to the entries in their reading notebooks where they had defined reading a few days earlier. She asked them to look at their earlier definition of reading and to write what they were thinking about it now. (See Figure 4.3.) The students were beginning to realize that reading was so much more than just "getting the words right."

Early in the year, it is the hard thinking we do around easy texts that sets the stage for future learning. Lessons like this invite kids to redefine reading for themselves and to continue to think about what reading means to them.

Figure 4.3 Courtney changes her definition of reading.

Literary Connections

We also want students to begin to appreciate the literary connections in their world. We want them to be part of the community of readers beyond

Students keep an eye out for literary connections to add to the board.

their classroom and the school walls. For example, we often see cartoons in the paper that relate to stories or fairy tales. We recently found a card with a picture of three bears and a little blonde girl on the front. The card says, "Happy Birthday, Oldilocks." We have seen ads for mortgage companies that show the three little pigs building houses. These types of things are part of our daily lives, and they remind us how much a part reading plays in them. We keep our eyes open for these things so that when the time is right, we can share them with our students. In an early issue of *Time for Kids,* one of the students spotted an article about a very large pig. There was a picture accompanying the article whose caption read, "Some pig!" Another student immediately noticed the connection to *Charlotte's Web* by E. B. White. This connection led us to set up a new bulletin board in the classroom for the children to display similar items. Throughout the year, they were on the lookout for literary connections. They found them in newspapers, books, and magazines.

Good Readers Get Stuck

> When I get totally confused in a book, my friends tell me all these ways to help me. So when that happens again, I know how to understand what I am reading.
> Julie

One of the first things we want upper elementary readers to understand is that good readers get stuck. Most of our students believe that reading is about getting the words right, and that if they get all of the words right (quickly!), they are good readers. They don't realize that all good readers get stuck in their reading. We need to help our students understand that experienced readers have strategies to help them get unstuck and that readers who instinctively know what to do when they get stuck are good readers.

Our goal for students in upper elementary classrooms is for them to become strategic readers. In *Strategies That Work: Teaching Comprehension to Enhance Understanding,* Stephanie Harvey and Anne Goudvis (2000) define strategic reading as "thinking about reading in ways that enhance learning and understanding" (p. 16). They and other educators at the Public Education and Business Coalition in Denver began to focus on the strategies proficient readers use, as identified by researchers. For example, P. David Pearson et al. (1992) identified the most critical strategies that readers use when they construct meaning from text. In *Mosaic of Thought* (1997), Ellin Keene and Susan Zimmerman describe the thought processes of proficient readers and the strategies that help children become more flexible, adaptive, independent, and engaged readers. They consider visualization to be among the comprehension strategies because proficient readers visualize and create images to help them understand what they read.

Here are some of the strategies proficient readers use:

- They make connections between what they know and the texts they read.
- They ask questions as they read.
- They visualize to enhance their understanding.
- They draw inferences during and after reading.
- They determine the most essential ideas in the text.
- They synthesize information.
- They monitor, correct, and clarify their understanding.

Stephanie Harvey and Anne Goudvis (2000) write, "Comprehension means that readers think not only about what they are reading but what they are understanding. When readers construct meaning, they are building their store of knowledge. But along with knowledge must come understanding" (p. 9). We have had many conversations with Cris Tovani, author of *I Read It, but I Don't Get It: Comprehension Strategies for Adolescent Readers* (2000), and Debbie Miller, author of *Reading with Meaning: Teaching Comprehension in the Primary Grades* (2002), about the kinds of teaching and learning that encourage strategic reading. We know that we need to do more than teach comprehension strategies in order for students to apply them independently.

We realized early on that students aren't often aware of what works for them or when they need to stop reading to clarify meaning. They know the comprehension strategies and can talk to us about them. They can tell us they are making a connection or making an inference, but they don't always know how and when to use that strategy when reading difficult texts independently.

For some of our students, strategy instruction will be new to them. Others may know the strategies, but are unable to use them when needed to help them understand what they read. They can make a connection to a text, but they do not necessarily make connections that help them understand the text at a deeper level. They can make a prediction, but not one that is likely to happen based on what they have already read in the story.

When we teach reading strategies as a daily lesson, checking skills off as we go, our students suffer. But when we think about the year as a whole and the kinds of behaviors and habits we want our students to have when they leave us, it is easier to see what is truly essential. We want our students to see the joy in reading and to become lifelong readers. But many young readers have come to see reading as a chore because it is not purposeful or because they do not have the strategies and behaviors in place to understand the types of texts they are encountering.

We've asked many young readers in grades 3–6 what they do when they get stuck. Almost all of them talk about getting stuck at the word level. They say that getting stuck means getting to a word they don't know. But in upper elementary grades, getting stuck means more than not knowing a word. As students begin to encounter more complex texts, meaning may break down beyond the word level. Getting stuck in their reading means many more things in the upper elementary grades. We've learned from Cris Tovani (2000) that older readers may:

- Daydream while reading (getting to the bottom of the page not knowing what they just read).
- Lose track of the characters as they come up again in the story.
- Get confused by the format or structure of the text.
- Fail to recognize when the setting or narrator has changed.
- Not be able to infer the less literal meaning in the text.
- Not pause in their reading to ask questions and monitor their comprehension.

Students need to know that they will always get stuck in their reading, but that throughout the year, they will be learning strategies for getting unstuck. Cris Tovani (2000) tells her students, "A strategy . . . is an intentional plan that readers use to help themselves make sense of their reading. Strategies are flexible and can be adapted to meet the demands of the reading task. Good readers use lots of strategies to help themselves make sense of text" (p. 5).

A great way to start a conversation about reading strategies, we have found, is to begin a chart that lists ways that students got stuck when they were learning how to read. We then use the chart to contrast those early reading experiences with the ways students get stuck in their reading now. After writing their own ideas down in their reading notebooks (see Figure 4.4), one fourth-grade class created the following chart:

Good Readers Get Stuck

Then	*Now*
Said the wrong words	Read too fast and don't know what happened
Didn't know a word	
Bigger words	Not concentrating on the book
Skipped words or sentences	Get distracted
Didn't understand	Too tired
Confused	Skip paying attention for a couple pages (this doesn't make sense!)
Couldn't find books I'd like	
Distracted	Words you don't know
Read things over and over	Don't know what it means

Didn't pay attention to detail	Reading names
	Lose my place
	Change in setting

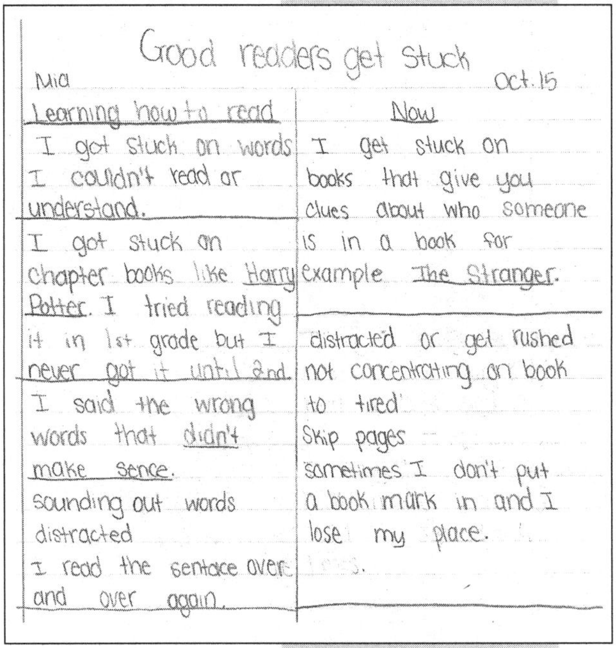

Good readers get stuck

Mia Oct. 15

Learning how to read	Now
I got stuck on words I couldn't read or understand.	I get stuck on books that give you clues about who someone is in a book for example The Stranger.
I got stuck on chapter books like Harry Potter. I tried reading it in 1st grade but I never got it until 2nd.	distracted or get rushed not concentrating on book to tired Skip pages sometimes I don't put a book mark in and I lose my place.
I said the wrong words that didn't make sence. sounding out words distracted I read the sentace over and over again.	

Figure 4.4 One student's notes on getting stuck.

Once students realize that good readers get stuck, they will be more open to the strategies needed to understand difficult texts. If we want our students to practice strategies that will help them when they do not understand, we must first make it okay for them to get stuck. We have found that students welcome this piece of learning. They are always relieved to find that they aren't the only ones who get stuck in their reading. These lessons are critical; they show students that being a good reader doesn't mean "getting all the words right," and they help them see how much more complicated higher-level reading can be.

By the end of the first few weeks of school, students have redefined reading and understand that all readers get stuck sometimes. They have learned that throughout the year reading will be important and that their lives as readers matter. We can then move on to the following broad goals for the rest of the year:

Having students continue to think about themselves as readers.
Having them begin to identify reading that is difficult.
Having them learn to support their thinking with evidence from the text.
Getting them to extend and sustain conversations during read-aloud.
Having them use their reading notebooks in increasingly sophisticated ways.
Helping them to develop new skills in selecting texts.

Because we know that these goals will be the foundation for many other lessons throughout the year, we launch into them slowly. Instead of jumping in with difficult texts and teaching children strategies for getting through them, we have students spend weeks paying attention to the kinds of reading that are difficult for them. They begin to realize that different texts are difficult for different readers, and they become able to identify the kinds of texts that they struggle with.

We notice behaviors in the first weeks of school that can make a big difference throughout the year. When one group of students began to read each day, we noticed that they spent several minutes flipping through their book.

After a few conversations, we realized that most of these students were reading novels without using bookmarks! This was an easy fix. Reminding kids about bookmarks and showing them how index cards and sticky notes can serve as bookmarks took just a few minutes. This is an example of why we can never stop observing our students carefully. This simple lesson gave students several more minutes of actual reading time each day.

We always go into a bit of a panic in mid-October. Up to then, we have been patient and have spent long periods of time having great conversations with students about reading, but then we realize it is almost November, and we fear that our students haven't accomplished anything. So we try to take some time in October to figure out what our students have learned. We invariably realize that they have accomplished quite a bit (thank goodness!). And we know exactly where to go next with instruction.

For example, this past fall, by mid-October, Franki's fourth-grade students had learned many things. They knew that:

> They could think and talk about their lives as readers.
> They could think about how they were changing as readers.
> Reading is about understanding, not merely getting the words right.
> Different readers like different books, but readers behave in similar ways.
> All readers struggle with some text.
> Getting stuck now is different than getting stuck while they were learning to read.
> They could identify easy and difficult texts.
> There are strategies to use when the text was difficult.
> Textbook reading is difficult for most students.
> Features in the textbook are intended to support the reader.
> Authors leave clues in the text to help with understanding.
> Conversations around books help readers think of ideas they wouldn't think of on their own.
> Readers choose books in different ways.

At this point, after taking stock and realizing that our students have learned a great deal about reading, we make a new list of goals for the following several weeks. Franki knew she would continue to work with her students on strategies for understanding hard text, supporting thinking with evidence from the text, and choosing good books. She also had some new goals, which were related to the following observations:

- Many of her students talked about "reading it again," but doing so didn't seem to be improving their comprehension.

- During conversations, many students were still just taking turns talking, instead of building on things others had said to deepen their understanding.
- Students were not remembering to write in their reading logs—so Franki thought they would need to be changed to daily logs.
- Students made predictions in order to be "right." They did not see how predictions, whether right or wrong, could help them understand the text better.

Working on these issues involves ambitious goals, but these new goals are attainable over the course of the year. And they all fit into the standards that the state and district establish. We know that if we help students learn to reread in different ways and to predict in ways that will enhance their understanding, they can use these skills when reading any text.

The stakes are high. Our students are going to be asked to perform at higher levels than we have asked them to do up to now. But we know that it is possible for them to do so—that our students constantly exceed even our highest expectations. If we look at the whole year and think about the over-all goals we have for our children, it is easier to teach well. And if we remember these goals, a slow but deliberate start always pays off in the long run. Yes, we know that by late fall, we will always panic, thinking we haven't taught anything. But we force ourselves to sit down each year and remind ourselves how far our students have come. And at the same time we need to keep the end of the year in sight so that we remain aware of where our students can go if we take it slow and give them more ownership and more responsibility for their learning.

CHAPTER 5

Grouping Beyond Levels

I heard other people sharing their thinking and it helped me to build on my thinking.
        Jordan

We're in a busy reading workshop one morning in March in Franki's fourth-grade classroom. Franki gathers a group of four students together to talk about how to recognize a change in setting as they read. She knows these particular students struggle with this issue in their independent reading because of the conversations she has had with them during individual conferences. Before she begins working with the group, she announces to the rest of the class, "This is a group that is going to work on finding clues for when the setting changes in a story. Who else thinks they need to join us?" From across the room a boy calls out that he wants to join the group. Another girl walks over and silently joins the circle as Franki begins to talk with them about changes in setting and hands out texts to read. Together, the group starts finding places in the text where they get confused about the setting, and looks for clues in the text that would signal a change in setting.

Our goal is to be at this point by March in our reading workshops. At this point, we are using assessments and observations of our students to know what skills to focus on in groups. We have goals for each of our students, and our students know enough about their own needs as readers to join a group that is working on a reading skill that they too need help with. Through instruction, planning, assessment, and observation, we have come to know our students well enough to match what our students need with what we teach. There is a comfortable, relaxed feel to our whole-group instruction, the flexible groups form and change regularly, and the individual conferences result in productive conversations with students about their reading.

We make better instructional decisions when we know our students well. Before our discussions later in this chapter about planning lessons and organizing groups, we begin with our beliefs about assessment, planning, and instruction in upper elementary classrooms.

A Close Look at Two Readers

As we mentioned earlier, our district requires us to give the Developmental Reading Assessment (DRA) in order to gain insights about our students as readers. This assessment tool has students choose a book, make predictions about the book, read the book, and respond to it. Teachers take a running record of each child reading and listen to his or her retelling of the story to determine an accurate level of comprehension. The DRA is an excellent assessment tool that provides some direction for teachers as they plan instruction. But it is just one piece of information about our students as readers.

Recently, we had conversations with two students, Anthony and Sarah, each of whom measured at level 40 on the DRA scale. If we considered only the level from this assessment tool to plan instruction, we might place both students in the same group and assume they needed the same instruction. In addition to administering the DRA, however, we also interviewed each student. The interviews were simply informal chats. We didn't sit with a clipboard of questions next to us and check them off as we asked them, though we did have a list of questions as a guide. These questions included the following:

How would you describe yourself as a reader?
What are you currently reading?
What kinds of things do you like to read?
What kinds of things do you *not* like to read?
What are you going to read next?
How do you choose the books you read?
What do you do when you get stuck?
What do you do when you start to read each day?
How do you keep track of the characters in the books you are reading?
What kind of reading is easy for you?
What kind of reading is hard for you?

These questions help us discover more about the strengths, habits, attitudes, and needs of our students. Early in the year, we do not ask students to read aloud to us. We wait a few weeks until they have realized that reading is about more than getting the words right. If we were to ask our students to read aloud to us before we had time to learn about the other aspects of their reading, we would reinforce the notion that our main goal for them as readers is oral fluency. Although fluency is important, it is not the only goal, and certainly not the most important one for older readers.

These conversations give us crucial information that we use to plan instruction, and they continue all year long. We match what we learn about individual students' interests and histories in reading with what we know about skills that are essential for upper elementary students to acquire. We try to heed Shelley Harwayne's (2002) advice: "Make sure you can articulate why you're doing what you're doing. Our time with students is precious and never enough. We can't waste time on things that don't add up, that don't connect to students' assessed needs and their interests. Teachers must remain decision-makers, making wise choices based on professional know-how" (p. 21).

We present this look at two readers to show how different students can be in their behaviors, tastes, interests, and abilities, even when they are reading at the same "level."

Anthony

Anthony began our interview by saying, "I like to read history and fiction. I read history to learn more about the past, and I read fiction to see how life is in other books." Anthony was a child who didn't necessarily read a variety of genres, but when we asked him what he was thinking about reading next, he said, "I might read some poetry, but I'm not sure what book or poet."

Anthony told us that when he gets stuck in his reading, he sounds words out, looks them up in a dictionary, skips the word, or fills in substitute words. He told us proudly, "Some of the history books I read are like grown-up books." When he begins a new book, he checks the back of the book for a summary. He opens the book to the first page and reads it. If he doesn't get stuck, he reads another page. He said, "Sometimes I read as many as ten pages and the back of the book before I decide to read the book." When he reads books with several characters in them, he writes the characters down on a piece of paper as they come into the story. He said, "Sometimes I write things by the names of the characters to help me remember who they are."

Anthony said he has strategies he uses when he starts reading each day to help him sustain comprehension over time. He told us, "When I start reading each day, I go back and read the last page I read before to remember what happened and how it happened." He told us that when he finishes reading each day, he tries to stop at the end of a chapter. He looks ahead to the next chapter title and the pictures to get an idea of what the chapter might be about. He told us, "In second grade and at the beginning of third grade, my favorite author was Marc Brown." He was currently reading *Wayside School Gets a Little Stranger* by Louis Sachar.

We were glad to know that Anthony had set a short-term reading goal for himself. We noticed that Anthony only recognized getting stuck at the word level. We began to think about which poetry books Anthony might enjoy that we could recommend to him.

Sarah

Sarah had been reading a few of the Pinky and Rex books by James Howe. In addition, she had recently read *Pirates Don't Wear Pink Sunglasses* and *Santa Doesn't Mop Floors* by Debbie Dadey. Sarah said, "I don't like to read thick books." When she chooses a book to read, she looks at the title to see if it sounds interesting, and she looks at the cover and the back of the book. Sarah said, "The Pinky and Rex books are average for me. Books with one sentence on a page are easy, and books with no pictures are hard." When we asked her about keeping track of characters as she reads, Sarah said, "I like books with only a couple of characters because it is easy to keep track of them." She said that when she gets stuck, she looks for chunks or small words inside words or she sounds the words out. She never reads on when she is stuck on a word. When she starts reading each day, she starts right where she left off. She doesn't go back to think about what she had read the day before. Sarah said, "I don't like to read. I would rather draw." Her favorite authors were Dr. Seuss and David Wisniewski.

Our interview with Sarah led us to believe that she was not very interested in reading and that she did not seem very confident as a reader. Our immediate goal would be to help Sarah gain confidence and begin to see herself as a reader.

Instructional Implications

After interviewing these two readers, we quickly determined that grouping them together for instruction would probably not be the most effective use of their time. They don't need the same kind of support, or even the same degree of teacher involvement.

While we use our conversations with students to help us plan instruction, we also want the conversations to help students identify their own strengths and needs in reading. Children can know all the best strategies for comprehending texts, but if they don't use them as they read, their understanding will falter. As Regie Routman (2003) reminds us, "Just because we teach our students strategies doesn't mean they apply them. They can 'do' the strategy, but they don't apply it when they read" (p. 120). Children should recognize who they are as readers. It helps them understand how every one of their reading experiences sharpens their skills and moves them forward. Once they know themselves as readers, they can begin to take some responsibility for planning and assessing what they need next from us and from their classmates.

Limitations of Levels

If we were using the guided reading levels as a planning tool for instruction for Sarah and Anthony, we might choose a book that is a level Q or R. But after getting to know Sarah and Anthony, we don't believe that basing instruction solely on book levels is the best way to help students develop new skills.

As Irene Fountas and Gay Su Pinnell (2001) write, "Individual students cannot be categorized as, for example, 'Level M Readers.' Their background knowledge varies widely according to the experiences they have had at home, in the community, and in school. Their reading ability develops along many dimensions" (p. 225). To plan effective instruction, we not only need to know the readers well, we also need to know the materials. By knowing our readers and our books, we will be better able to help students choose books that will help them grow as readers.

We worry about the level mania that is occurring across the country. It doesn't matter whether teachers are using guided reading levels, Accelerated Reading® levels, or some other leveling system. Students and teachers in the upper elementary grades often measure progress in inappropriate ways. We worry that our children will not choose books because they are interesting or challenging, but simply because they are the "right" level. Students sometimes define reading as "getting through a book at my level" rather than enjoying and understanding great texts.

We've spent a lot of time looking at leveled books. Think for a moment about the strategies and behaviors that cannot be measured by a test or an assessment instrument but need to be taught to students in the upper elementary grades. As Jo Worthy and Misty Sailors (2001) write: "We have often seen these [leveled] lists used in place of teacher judgment and have heard teachers describe students' reading in terms of numbers (e.g., "He's a level 21") rather than in ways that reflect the complexity of reading. Further, moving students step by step through text difficulty levels assumes that students progress in small, measured increments" (p. 232).

Let's take a look at two books that are a Level Q on the guided reading list (Fountas and Pinnell 2001, Appendix 61). Although these books are the same level, they offer different supports and challenges.

Bunnicula by James Howe Longer text that requires sustained comprehension over time.	*Grandpa's Face* by Eloise Greenfield Can be read in one or two sittings. Realistic fiction. Illustrations support the text.

Fantasy genre.	Two main characters throughout the story.
Very few illustrations to support the text.	
Several characters to remember throughout the story.	

Although Anthony would probably be successful with both of these books, Sarah may not yet have the skills needed to stick with a longer novel like *Bunnicula.* Instead, we might want her to try a book like *Judy Moody* by Megan McDonald, which has each character's picture listed in the front of the book. A book like this would help Sarah begin to read longer novels, which seem to be a stumbling block for her. *Judy Moody* provides the support of a character chart and can build Sarah's confidence as a reader. We also think that the humor in this book might appeal to Sarah; it might be a series that she could get hooked on.

Because Sarah's needs are similar to those of some of the other students in the class, it makes sense for us to put her in a group with those other students—for example, students who are struggling with keeping track of characters in their reading. Anthony's greatest need, however, is unique, so it makes sense to meet with him individually. Our focus is on what we can do to help each reader rather than making sure that everyone is in a small group. We guide and support our upper elementary readers in many ways besides assigning them to reading groups.

Levels are just one tool in a large array of assessments that can help us to plan instruction. Once we have completed the informal reading interviews, we administer more formal assessments, such as the DRA. We also continue to observe students, have individual conferences, and review past test scores. This past year, as she discovered insights about each student over six to eight weeks, Franki collected the information on a grid. (That form is provided in the appendix; a completed sample grid is shown in Figure 5.1.)

Strategy Lesson: Keeping Track of Characters

Why We Teach It: As students encounter more complex texts, one of the biggest challenges for them is to keep track of the characters when there are more than a few in the story. They often get confused, mix up one character with another, or continue reading when they know they have lost track of who everyone is in the story.

Possible Anchor Book: *Judy Moody Was in a Mood. Not a Good Mood. A Bad Mood,* by Megan McDonald. This is one of two Judy Moody books published by Candlewick Press. The second is *Judy Moody Gets Famous.*

Figure 5.1 Franki's grid.

Name	Interview	Observation	DRA	Survey	Standardized Tests	Goal
Beth	disliked reading last year / trying to enjoy reading again / picky about what she reads	reads at recess / always very engaged	Level 50 / good comprehension and reflection / has had no strategy instruction but uses strat. naturally	likes fantasy and popular titles	well above grade level	book choice / strategy instruction / set own reading goals
Cameron	"safe" reading / likes funny, scary, small books / difficulty with unknown words	very conscientious / little risk taking	Level 38 / goes on when text doesn't make sense / plan/plane (miscue)	Bailey School Kids / Henry Huggins / interested in the solar system	just at grade level	confidence / expand reading choices / take risks when stuck
Anthony	likes history and nonfiction / good previewing skills / keeps track of characters	engaged during reading / brings books from home	Level 40 / very few miscues / good comprehension	reads only nonfiction / no favorite authors	above grade level	poetry (Anthony's goal)
Doug	likes zoo animal books / wants "hard" books / "I don't get stuck"	chooses very difficult books / distracted and unengaged during reading time	Level 38 / very few miscues / very little comprehension	likes Harry Potter, Lord of the Ring / no favorite author	below grade level	know when he's stuck / choosing books (maybe short stories)
Sarah	likes Pinky and Rex / not interested in reading / likes series books with pictures	difficulty choosing books / not engaged / social during reading time	Level 40 / good comprehension / few miscues / fluent	doesn't like to read / favorite author Dr. Seuss	above grade level	ready to read more complex books / reading attitude
Stephanie	likes nonfiction series (Eyewitness) / perceives herself as a good reader	very social / moves from book to book	Level 40 / few miscues / adequate comprehension	wants to read Junie B Jones / has no goals for herself / "nothing to improve"	below grade level	goal setting / recognize when text is difficult

In both of these chapter books, there is a "who's who" page at the front of the book, containing a picture of all nine characters in the story along with their names. In *Judy Moody Gets Famous* the page also contains a brief description of each of the characters. This series is a good choice for children who are moving away from stories with just two or three characters in them.

How We Teach It: As students preview the book, it is important for them to discover the "who's who" page. We discuss how the page might be helpful as they read the story. As the group begins to read the book, we pause when a new character enters the story and refer to the "who's who" page. As they continue to read, we encourage the students to refer to this page when they are confused about any of the characters in the story.

Follow-Up: Once the children have read the book for a few days, we often ask them to reflect on how the "who's who" page was helpful for them. We have them share the list of characters they were keeping as they read. We ask them what they learned that will help them the next time they are reading a book with several characters. We suggest that they keep a list of characters on a sticky note or a bookmark as they read. *Amelia's Notebook* by Marissa Moss is a great book to share. When Amelia moves to a new school, she draws pictures in her notebook of

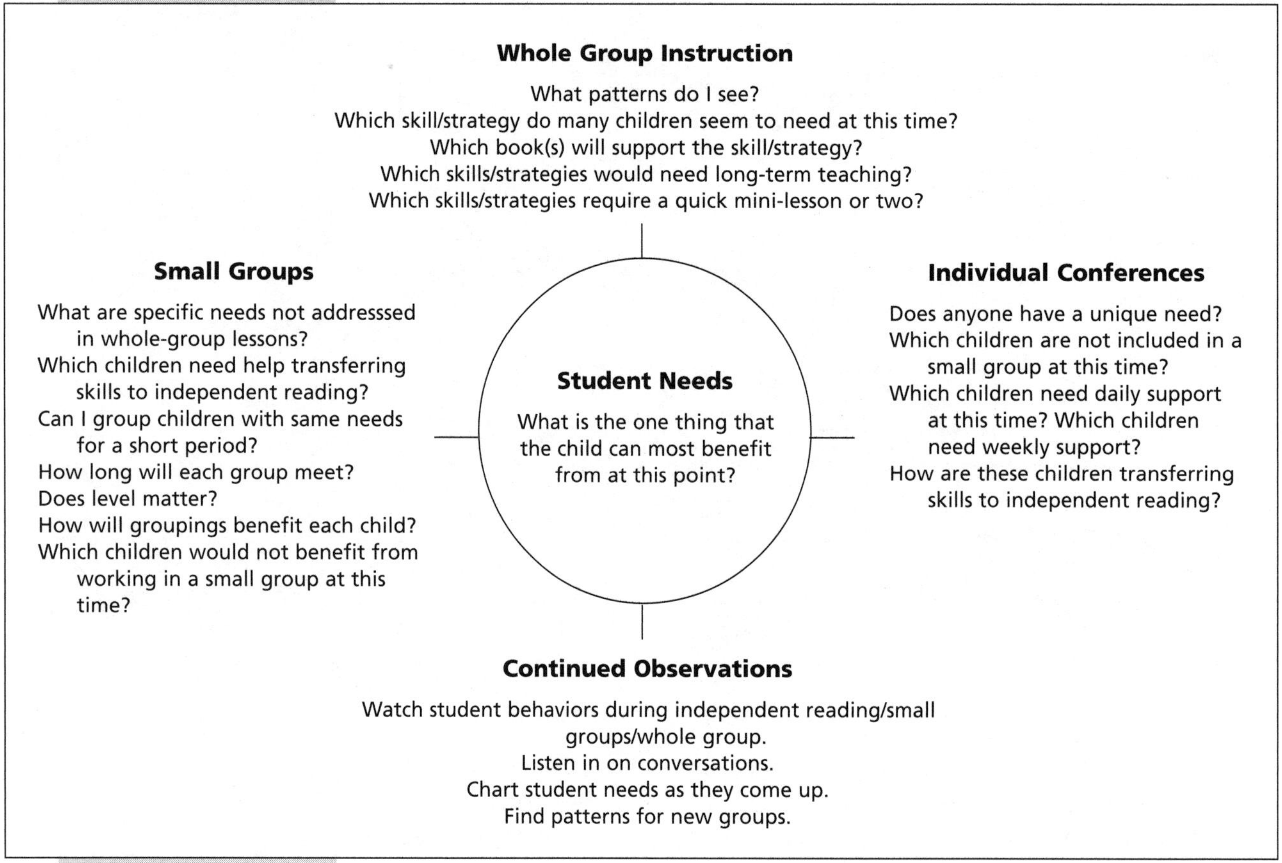

Whole Group Instruction

What patterns do I see?
Which skill/strategy do many children seem to need at this time?
Which book(s) will support the skill/strategy?
Which skills/strategies would need long-term teaching?
Which skills/strategies require a quick mini-lesson or two?

Small Groups

What are specific needs not addresssed in whole-group lessons?
Which children need help transferring skills to independent reading?
Can I group children with same needs for a short period?
How long will each group meet?
Does level matter?
How will groupings benefit each child?
Which children would not benefit from working in a small group at this time?

Student Needs

What is the one thing that the child can most benefit from at this point?

Individual Conferences

Does anyone have a unique need?
Which children are not included in a small group at this time?
Which children need daily support at this time? Which children need weekly support?
How are these children transferring skills to independent reading?

Continued Observations

Watch student behaviors during independent reading/small groups/whole group.
Listen in on conversations.
Chart student needs as they come up.
Find patterns for new groups.

Figure 5.2a Grouping for instruction.

the people she meets and writes about them. Students might want to do something similar in their reading logs.

Thinking Through Grouping

A planning form (see Figures 5.2a and b and the blank form in the appendix) often helps us with the instructional decisions we make. Some teachers have found it helpful to use such a form as part of their lesson plans. The form helps us to see the broad picture of our instruction that students will receive in whole-class, small-group, and individual instruction.

Whole-Group Instruction

We look for problems that many of the students in our class are having when we think about the whole-group instruction we want to provide. What skills

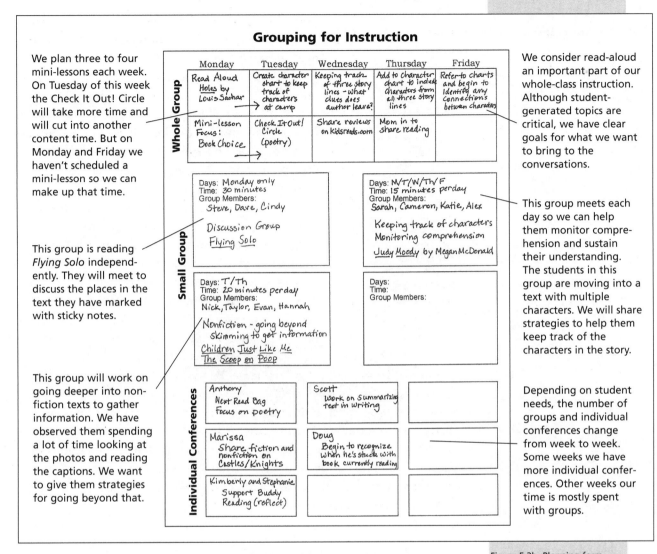

Grouping for Instruction

We plan three to four mini-lessons each week. On Tuesday of this week the Check It Out! Circle will take more time and will cut into another content time. But on Monday and Friday we haven't scheduled a mini-lesson so we can make up that time.

This group is reading *Flying Solo* independently. They will meet to discuss the places in the text they have marked with sticky notes.

This group will work on going deeper into non-fiction texts to gather information. We have observed them spending a lot of time looking at the photos and reading the captions. We want to give them strategies for going beyond that.

We consider read-aloud an important part of our whole-class instruction. Although student-generated topics are critical, we have clear goals for what we want to bring to the conversations.

This group meets each day so we can help them monitor comprehension and sustain their understanding. The students in this group are moving into a text with multiple characters. We will share strategies to help them keep track of the characters in the story.

Depending on student needs, the number of groups and individual conferences change from week to week. Some weeks we have more individual conferences. Other weeks our time is mostly spent with groups.

Whole Group

	Monday	Tuesday	Wednesday	Thursday	Friday
	Read Aloud *Holes* by Louis Sachar	Create character chart to keep track of characters at camp	Keeping track of three story lines – what clues does author leave?	Add to character chart to include characters from all three story lines	Refer to charts and begin to identify any connections between characters
	Mini-lesson Focus: Book Choice	Check It Out! Circle (poetry)	Share reviews on Kidsreads.com	Mom in to share reading	

Small Group

Days: Monday only
Time: 30 minutes
Group Members: Steve, Dave, Cindy

Discussion Group
Flying Solo

Days: M/T/W/Th/F
Time: 15 minutes per day
Group Members: Sarah, Cameron, Katie, Alex

Keeping track of characters
Monitoring comprehension
Judy Moody by Megan McDonald

Days: T/Th
Time: 20 minutes per day
Group Members: Nick, Taylor, Evan, Hannah

Nonfiction – going beyond skimming to get information
Children Just Like Me
The Scoop on Poop

Days:
Time:
Group Members:

Individual Conferences

Anthony
Next Read Bag
Focus on poetry

Marissa
Share fiction and nonfiction on Castles/Knights

Kimberly and Stephanie
Support Buddy Reading (reflect)

Scott
Work on summarizing text in writing

Doug
Begin to recognize when he's stuck with book currently reading

Figure 5.2b Planning form.

and strategies do many of the children seem to need at this time? Which text or texts will support the skill or strategy? What skills and strategies will we need to teach over a long period of time, and which will require just a quick mini-lesson or two? We look for patterns in the classroom that will help us plan whole-group instruction. Our whole-class lessons should always be based on what we have learned about our students as readers.

Early in the year, we often find that learning how to choose books and how to browse are the most common needs we see in our students. Other early challenges for many students include knowing when they are stuck, sustaining interest or comprehension, and writing in response to reading. Early in the year, students' needs seem more similar than they do later in the year. Students' needs become more individual as the year goes on and as we get to

Some Whole-Class Lessons We Have Taught

Time	Strategy/Skill	Text Used
Early in year	What makes text hard?	*Time for Kids*
Early in year	Self as reader	*Reading Grows* by Ellin B. Senisi
Early in year	Book choice	Variety of books
Midyear	Using evidence	*The Table Where Rich People Sit* by Byrd Baylor
Midyear	Keeping track of characters	*Holes* by Louis Sachar
Midyear	Understanding powerful writing	*Because of Winn-Dixie* by Kate DiCamillo
Midyear	Rereading for understanding	*Emma's Rug* by Allen Say
End of year	Reading multiple sources	Various newspapers
End of year	Author study	*The Tiger Rising* by Kate DiCamillo

know our students better. Thus, we often spend more time on whole-class instruction early in the year and more time with small groups later in the year.

We are careful not to try to teach too much in one mini-lesson. We focus on a particular skill, strategy, or behavior that we know will move our readers forward. We combine our knowledge of the children with what we know about experienced readers to determine what will help our students become more strategic in their reading.

We don't want to spend so much time with whole-group lessons that we cut into our students' independent reading time. It is tempting to short-change independent reading time in order to teach a necessary skill. We try to remember that reading develops over days, weeks, and months, and that the best thing we can do for our students is to give them time to practice during independent reading time.

Specific skills and strategies that good readers use need to be taught. As Stephanie Harvey (1998) writes in her book *Nonfiction Matters: Reading, Writing, and Research in Grades 3–8*, "For too many years, we simply asked students to perform without showing them how, and then expressed disappointment at the less-than-hoped-for results" (p. 64). We can no longer be satisfied with giving our students a list of questions or a packet of comprehension activities to complete after their reading. We know that we need to help them learn what to do *during* their reading of a text in order for them to understand it.

Small-Group Instruction

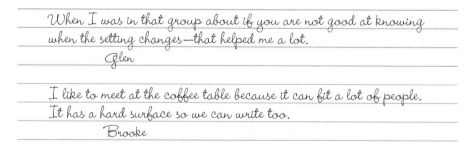

When I was in that group about if you are not good at knowing when the setting changes—that helped me a lot.
Glen

I like to meet at the coffee table because it can fit a lot of people. It has a hard surface so we can write too.
Brooke

We used to worry about needing to see children a certain number of times each week or making sure that every child was in a small group each week. Now we make decisions based on what the children need rather than the unfounded pressures we've put upon ourselves.

Flexible grouping provides a framework for meeting the needs of each reader in a systematic way. Just like Sarah and Anthony, each student comes to us with a unique array of skills, behaviors, attitudes, and reading experiences. Sometimes we have to resist the urge to teach a concept or skill just because we know it is in the curriculum or we know it will be measured on a test. As Regie Routman (2003) reminds us, "Instead of focusing on 'Is it right?' or 'What's the best way?' let's think about and focus on what's right and best for a particular student or group of students at this point in time as indicated by what we've read, the conversations we've had with our colleagues, valid research we've consulted, our teaching experiences, and our students' needs and interests" (p. 6).

When we plan small-group instruction, we look for patterns that emerge within groups of students. We look for several students who might benefit from the same type of instruction and group children who have similar needs. We think about the support small-group instruction can provide for our students and how they will benefit from reading and learning together. Is there a group of children with the same needs that can meet for a short time? Are there children who need help transferring skills to independent reading? As we plan for small groups, we think about how often and how long we will meet with each group. We think about whether or not the level of the text we use matters. We think about how the way we group children will benefit each child in the group.

We have no formula for the number of days, length of time, or size of groups when we plan small-group instruction. Some weeks, several groups are going on at the same time. Other weeks, we spend more time with individual students in conferences. We try to remain focused on what the children need, and we are flexible with the groups.

For a group of children who have trouble choosing books, we might meet with them for one or two days until we feel that each has made a good choice and learned some strategies for choosing a book. For students who are working on understanding unfamiliar words, we might conduct small-group mini-lessons once a week for a few weeks. However, if we are meeting with a group that is having trouble sustaining comprehension over an entire novel, we would need to meet with them every day to scaffold their understanding throughout the entire text. We try to determine what is the best use of time for our students and how to create a schedule that allows us to facilitate their learning.

Although we are often the ones to decide on the purpose and members of a group, we also ask for student input. We want children to be involved in their own learning, and we know that they often know themselves better

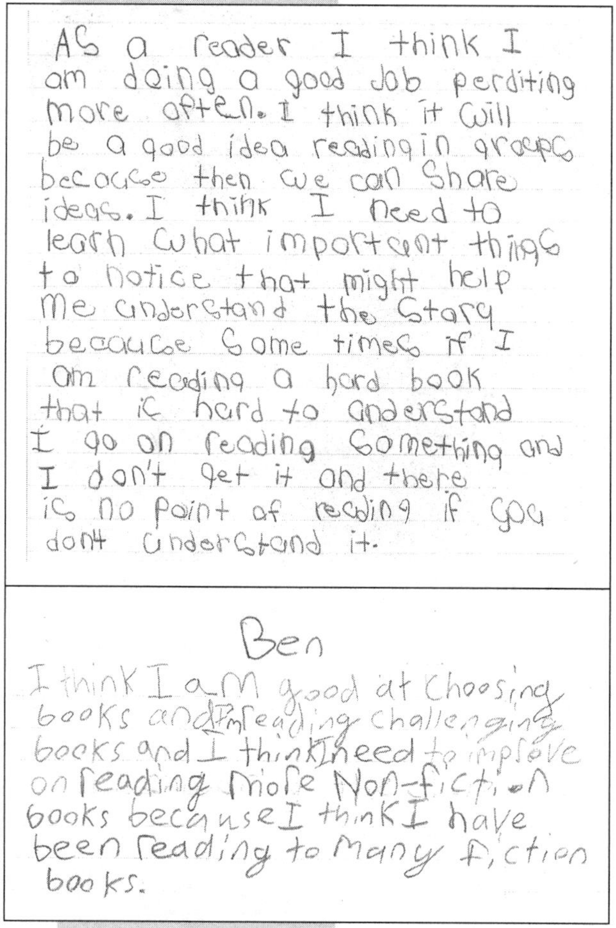

> As a reader I think I am doing a good job perditing more often. I think it will be a good idea reading in groups because then we can share ideas. I think I need to learn what important things to notice that might help me understand the story because some times if I am reading a hard book that is hard to understand I go on reading something and I don't get it and there is no point of reading if you don't understand it.

> **Ben**
>
> I think I am good at choosing books and reading challenging books and I think I need to improve on reading more Non-fiction books because I think I have been reading to many fiction books.

Figure 5.3 Casey and Ben reflect on ways that group work may help.

than we do. So a few times each year, we ask our students to think about whether they would benefit from being part of a group and to let us know what they think they need to learn. We ask them to think about which reading skills they feel they need more instruction on and which skills, strategies, and behaviors they would learn best as part of a small group. (See Figure 5.3.)

Early in the year, we may give our students some options during this discussion. We may say that we are thinking of offering groups on reading nonfiction, choosing books, and keeping track of characters. We personally invite those students who we know would benefit from the instruction. Then we open it up to others who are interested. As the year progresses, we leave the decisions about groups more open-ended, and students often tell us what lessons they need. When students tell us what they think they need to learn, their thoughts often match ours exactly! And if children ask to be in a group, they are often much more engaged and committed.

Individual Instruction

We also look for students who have needs that will not be met in the whole-class and small-group lessons, and we make time to meet with those students individually. When we know our students as individuals and take the time to build profiles of them as readers, we are much better prepared to meet with them individually about their reading. As we think about the children in our class, we look for the ones who have unique needs because we want to consider what we can do in an individual conference that will support them. We consider those children who need daily support. Which children might benefit from a brief conference every day—one that leaves them prepared to engage in reading for the day and gives them the support they need? Which ones can move along with weekly support? Individual conferences give us opportunities to sharpen our image of the readers in our classrooms.

Looking at the planning chart (Figure 5.2b), we intend to meet with Marissa, who is disengaged as a reader but has recently shown an interest in castles and knights. We plan to introduce her to a selection of nonfiction books that would interest her. We also intend to meet with Doug. He doesn't always know what to do when he is stuck in his reading. We plan to show him several strategies for understanding difficult text.

We continually observe, talk, and listen to the children in our class. We watch them during independent reading and in small- and large-group lessons. We listen in on conversations. We consider the needs of each of our students and find patterns for new groups, and the cycle continues. Our thinking in response to what we know about our students is what helps us plan for short-term instruction and long-term teaching. We recognize what skills we can teach quickly and what strategies will take more time for our readers to develop, and we always have a clear picture of where we are going with our teaching in response to what we know about our children as readers.

What Instruction Does the Child Receive?

We often get overwhelmed by the management issues involved in grouping. We worry that all students aren't in a group or that we don't meet individually with one child as often as another. We need to think of our planning from the student's eyes. When we plan for whole-group, small-group, and individual instruction, we try to think about what each child will experience. How will his or her week look?

For example, we have decided that Sarah will benefit from all whole-group lessons. She has difficulty choosing books, and the mini-lessons dedicated to this will support her in her book choice. She will also benefit from the conversations in our read-aloud sessions. Even though these group lessons don't necessarily meet her immediate needs, they will support her as she becomes more sophisticated as a reader. Sarah will be part of a small group, but not part of individual conferences. This will guarantee that she has time each day to read independently. Sarah's days, planned this way, seem very balanced.

Anthony, too, will benefit from the whole-class lessons. The read-aloud could be powerful for him, and the book choice lessons will help him meet his own goal. Although he is not in a small group and we will only meet with him once this week, Anthony is at a point in his reading where we know he will spend his independent time well. He will have long periods of time each day to read independently. Because he isn't in a group or many individual conferences this week, we will make sure to pay close attention to his talk and his writing during whole-class lessons to determine what his next needs may be. Then we may put him in a group to help him meet the new need.

A Close-Up Look at Instructing a Skill in Whole-Class, Small-Group, and Individual Settings: Rereading for Understanding

I have been in a rereading group. I went there because I have had a hard time reading because I would read too fast and skip over some things. When I started rereading, I could understand the book better.

Karynn

One of the skills we want all of our students to develop is the ability to reread for understanding. Good readers reread, but they don't just read a passage again—they read it differently if they are to gain a deeper understanding. Regie Routman (2003) writes that "rereading is the strategy that is most useful to readers of all ages. When given opportunities to reread material, readers' comprehension always goes up. And research consistently shows that rereading is one of the most highly recommended strategies for struggling readers. Yet, we rarely teach rereading as a primary strategy" (p. 122).

Students will use rereading as a strategy throughout the school year. It will come up in whole-group, small-group, and individual conversations throughout the year. We use our first lessons on rereading to define it for our students and to give them the opportunity to see the power that it has. Because it is important for the whole class to have the same definitions and expectations for rereading, we always do the first several lessons on rereading with the entire class. Even students who reread successfully need to be made aware that this strategy will help them when they get to an unfamiliar genre and challenging text. We are also always on the lookout for books that encourage rereading. These are books in which a great deal of thinking is left up to the reader, books that don't end with a note of finality, so that when we finish them we still have lots of questions. *Emma's Rug* by Allen Say is the perfect book to use to teach students the power of rereading.

Understanding That Rereading Is Reading Differently

Books That Invite Rereading

The Summer My Father Was Ten by Pat Brisson
Annie and the Old One by Miska Miles
Jemma's Journey by Trevor Romain
Emma's Rug by Allen Say
Stranger in the Mirror by Allen Say
The Wretched Stone by Chris Van Allsburg

We might introduce the whole class to the concept of rereading through a read-aloud that includes focused writing and discussion. When we read *Emma's Rug* to Franki's fourth-grade class, we read it aloud three times. Before we read it the first time, we told the students that we would be reading it to them several times. We told them that this was a book that could be more deeply understood by rereading. We wanted them to feel the power of rereading for themselves, and to record some changes in their thinking in their reading notebooks as they reread the story.

On the first read, the students enjoyed the book, but were frustrated at the end because of all of the questions they still had. Following the first reading, we asked them to respond in their reading notebooks in any way that they wished. On the second day of this series of lessons, we asked our students to think about a place in the book that they wished they understood better. Blair said, "The thing that I didn't get was when she went outside and saw all her paintings and then the next day she started drawing again." Before we began to reread the book aloud, we asked the students how they would read (or listen) differently the second time. Blair wrote, "I'll be listening by thinking more creatively. I think she was imagining the drawings she drew before and that reminded her how fun it was to do art." After the second reading, Blair wrote, "This time, I actually saw the drawings all over the lawn and got to understand it better."

The children's responses were diverse. It was evident that they were beginning to understand the power of rereading. Shea mentioned that when we read the story for the first time, he was anticipating the end of the book. Since he now knew how the book ended, he could listen for other things. Tessa talked about how she wanted this time to focus only on those things dealing with the rug, since that was an important part of the book. The children also talked together about the story, so that they could learn from others' thinking. On the third day, we again asked them to use their notebooks to think about the way they would read (or listen) differently. (See Figure 5.4.)

Rereading a book like *Emma's Rug* helps students to understand that readers often have a different focus or purpose each time they reread. If we don't teach our students to stop before they reread and think about how the second or third reading will be different from the first, they may never find success in rereading. The power of rereading is in reading *differently*. *Emma's Rug* is a good anchor lesson for rereading. Throughout the year, when our students talk about reading again and reading differently, they often refer to *Emma's Rug*.

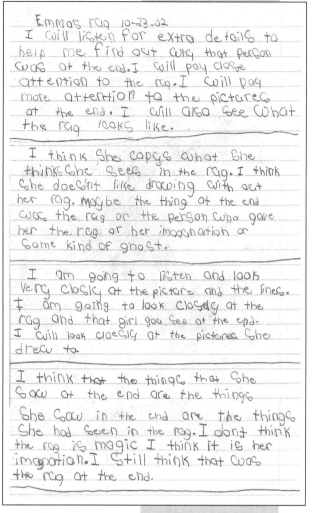

Figure 5.4 Casey tracks the changes in his thinking as he reads and rereads *Emma's Rug* by Alan Say.

At other times during the year, to support rereading during independent reading time, we might pull volunteers together into a group. We would look for students like Anthony, who we know is already rereading to support his reading—he told us that when he starts reading each day, he rereads the last page from the previous day. To form the group, we would ask which students find that rereading really helps them. This past year, a group of four volunteers met to discuss rereading. At the first meeting, the students chatted informally about rereading. They talked about the times rereading was helpful to them and times it wasn't. Sam said that rereading was helpful when he found he had read something too quickly. Brooke mentioned that she often rereads to find evidence in the text that she may have missed. Casey said that rereading did not often help him when he got to names he couldn't pronounce.

Then we gave each group member six arrow-shaped sticky notes (these can be purchased at office supply stores; they are often used when signatures are required on documents). We asked the students to keep the sticky notes handy as they read over the next several days. As they reread, we asked them to mark the places in their book where they reread so they could share them with the group.

The group met again about a week later to share what they had discovered:

- Sam said that he caught himself rereading a nonfiction book, *Ancient Rome* by Simon James. He read something that surprised him, so he reread the passage to make sure he had read it correctly.
- Brooke reread a line from *Mick Harte Was Here* by Barbara Park that didn't make sense to her. She reread the line and thought about the way the words were put together to figure out what the sentence meant.
- Kelsey reread the first page of the second chapter of a book about an animal hospital, because a new character was being introduced on that page. She had thought that the entire book would be about one character and then realized that a new character was going to be introduced in each new chapter.
- Casey reread a few pages of *Lewis and Clark* by George Sullivan when he started reading one day. He had not picked up the book for a few days and had forgotten what had happened. He read the previous few pages again to remind him of what had happened.

To encourage the rest of the class to begin using rereading as a strategy, we asked these four students to share their experiences with the class. Each child also made a small poster about their rereading for a class bulletin board. Other students in the class would add to the board as they found instances when rereading was helping them.

After this group shared their rereading experiences, we asked if there were any students in the class who felt that they weren't very good at rereading for understanding and could benefit from a group on rereading. Five students joined the group and began learning how to reread independently. (Sarah would benefit from joining a group on rereading; it might help her learn to reread to keep track of characters.)

Individual Conferences

Glen approached Franki a few days after he started to read *The Castle in the Attic* by Elizabeth Winthrop. He realized that the character of Mrs. Phillips kept coming up in the story and he didn't really know who she was. He said, "She keeps being mentioned a lot and I think that she is going to be an important character. I can't figure out who she is." Obviously, Glen had missed some of the clues in what he had read that would have told him who Mrs. Phillips was. After Glen and Franki had talked a bit, Franki gave him a stack of sticky notes and asked him to reread, looking for any mention of Mrs. Phillips—clues about the character. She asked him to meet with her the following day to discuss what he had figured out. Glen went back to his independent reading and marked sentences such as "Mrs. Phillips was waiting for William at the kitchen door" and "Mrs. Phillips had been with William's family since he was born." During the conference the following day, Franki and Glen read through all of the marked text and inferred that Mrs. Phillips was the housekeeper in the story. Because Glen had been part of whole-group instruction about rereading, he understood the power of rereading. But Glen's need was specific to his situation. For Glen to understand the book he was reading, he needed some support and scaffolding. This conference gave Glen a reason to use rereading for a specific purpose—a strategy that will help him with this book as well as future books.

Even when there were no specific lessons on rereading for the whole class or in small groups, rereading continued to be part of classroom conversations in read-aloud sessions, mini-lessons, and small groups. It is easy to build on conversations about rereading when the whole class has been involved in them. Throughout the year, we can add to the list of reasons students may find rereading to be helpful.

The decisions we make about whole-group, small-group, and individual instruction are challenging. If we want our students to know themselves and their needs we need to get them in a variety of groupings. We have often

Rereading with a Read-Aloud

Sometimes we read a book to our class that many of the students have previously read. We use this as an opportunity to teach strategies in rereading. In one class, several of the students had already read *Holes* by Louis Sachar before we read it to them. We met with these students before we started the book and asked them how this time might be different for them. Just as we did with *Emma's Rug*, we asked these readers to think about how they would read or listen differently based on questions they had after they had read it on their own. We charted their responses to remind them of what they could do while experiencing the book for a second time:

Pay attention to details.
Try to answer questions that weren't answered.
Try to understand parts we didn't get.
Listen for things we missed the first time.
Listen to the end—there was so much information in it.
Listen for any clues we missed leading to the surprise at the end.

found that students who are quiet in whole-class conversations come to life in a small group. Others are more comfortable in one-on-one settings. By thinking through individual students' needs, looking for patterns among students, and planning accordingly, teachers can enable students to benefit from a variety of instruction.

So Many Skills, So Little Time

There is only so much time in a school year. We constantly struggle with deciding how best to use that time so that our students can fulfill the expectations of the course of study for their grade level and meet the mandated standards for student achievement. Regie Routman (2003) reminds us to make every moment in the classroom count. She writes, "When I suggest that we need to 'teach with a sense of urgency' I'm not talking about teaching prompted by anxiety but rather about making every moment in the classroom count, about ensuring that our instruction engages students and moves them ahead, about using daily evaluation and reflection to make wise teaching decisions. Complacency will not get our students where they need to be. I am relaxed and happy when I am working with students, but I am also mindful of where I need to get them and how little time I have in which to do it. I teach each day with a sense of urgency" (p. 41).

It is tempting to make a list of all of the concepts and skills that our students need to learn and check them off as we teach them. But, these strategies are complex, and we expect our students to use them all their lives. We can't expect children to be able to use these strategies independently, without support, after just a few lessons. As teachers, we work to design whole-class, small-group, and individual experiences that model and scaffold our students' learning and give them the time they need to develop independence.

Threads of Learning Throughout the Year

When we focus on a few critical threads of learning throughout the year, our teaching becomes more purposeful. Our goal is to build on previous reading experiences and also to help students read a variety of genres and more complex texts with deeper understanding. The following threads of learning provide a focus for our teaching.

Conversations and Writing to Clarify Thinking

In her book *The Art of Teaching Reading,* Lucy Calkins (2000) states, "The mark of a good book talk is that people are not just reporting on ideas they've already had; they are, instead, generating ideas together" (p. 235). When students are able to use conversations and writing to express their thinking, their understanding deepens. We need to create opportunities for students to talk and write about the books they are reading and their experiences as readers to help them clarify their thinking and support their independence.

Browsing and Book Choice All Year Long

Students who know themselves well are more capable of choosing books, knowing when texts are easy or difficult, monitoring their comprehension, and sustaining their reading. When we help them become aware of who they are as readers, the skills, strategies, and behaviors that they learn will be applied to their independent reading.

Reading Difficult Texts with Persistence and Stamina

Students will continue to experience texts that are difficult for a variety of reasons throughout their lives. The texts may be difficult because of the topic, the writing style, or the genre. They may be difficult because the reader cannot concentrate due to something else going on in his or her life. The types of texts that are difficult for a reader will change. Our goal is for students to have the skills to recognize when text is hard for them and to be able to use strategies to construct meaning from the text.

Supporting Thinking with Evidence from the Text

If our students can defend their thinking about their reading by using evidence from the text, they will be able to think through most texts. Because students in grades 3–6 often have been exposed to reading strategy instruction, providing evidence asks them to go a step further. Often readers change their thinking as they read because of new information they find in the text. When readers make predictions and inferences, synthesize, or analyze, evidence from the text will give them confidence and credibility.

The chapters in Part Two discuss these threads of learning in detail.

CHAPTER 6

Conversations and Writing to Clarify Thinking

One day, I had a thought of something and when someone talked, it made me understand that my idea could not work.
    Kelsie

I can almost see my thinking because I write it on paper.
    Sam

In the middle of the year, Franki's fourth graders were working on independent research projects. During one of the mini-lessons, Franki was modeling on a chart a way for Trent to consider organizing his information about the Eiffel Tower. As she wrote on the chart, she wasn't sure how to spell "Eiffel." She asked Trent and he started with "I–F–E–." Franki said, "I think it starts with an *E*. Can you check it somewhere?" Several other students working nearby piped in, saying, "No, I'm pretty sure it's an *I* at the beginning." Franki asked Trent to find it in a book so they could write it correctly on the chart, as the other children continued to insist that the word started with an *I*. Thinking that this was a great time for a quick impromptu lesson on how one's life experiences can inform one's literacy, Franki said, "You know, I am pretty sure it starts with an *E*. I read about the Eiffel Tower quite a bit because I took French for five years." Chris said, "Yeah, but how long ago was *that*?" Amused, Franki realized just how comfortable her students had become in conversations with her about reading and writing.

We are all learners in the classroom, working together to extend our thinking and learn from the conversations we have with one another. These

Notebooks support conversations.

There are many opportunities for conversations.

conversations help our students reshape what they know about themselves as readers and give them the opportunity to develop the skills they need to become more competent readers. Writing in response to their reading experiences helps students clarify their thinking, develop new ideas, and recognize their unique qualities as readers. We can develop daily whole-class instruction to support and extend students' reading in a variety of ways through conversation and writing.

Rethinking Whole-Class Books and Read-Aloud

I like it when we sit in a circle during Read Aloud because you can see everyone and that way I know who is talking.
        Brooke

There are times when it is important for the whole class to read the same text because this common reading experience provides opportunities for shared conversations. However, we have never found a book that was the right match for every reader in the classroom at the same time. Although a book may be a good fit for most of the students in the class, it will probably be too difficult for a few. Also, reading a book together takes a huge amount of classroom time and often cuts into independent reading time. Rather than asking students to read the same book, we can better meet their needs through read-aloud. When our students are engaged in whole-class lessons, small-group discussions, and read-aloud, reading whole-class books together isn't a critical part of our reading time.

If we have a class set of the books, students can follow along as we read aloud.

In the past few years, we have revised the way we use our read-aloud time to meet the needs of a wider range of readers in our classroom. We knew that reading aloud to children is engaging and is often a favorite activity of both students and teachers. So we wanted to develop ways to use our read-aloud time even more effectively. We never want to change the feel of read-aloud time—we always want our students to approach read-aloud expecting to listen to a great story in a relaxed setting. Surprisingly, we have found that when we have something in mind that we want the children to learn during read-aloud time, and when we stop to chat and listen to children throughout our reading of the book, the children are even more engaged than they were before we put an instructional twist on read-aloud. Conversations and writing during read-aloud time draw our students deeper into the story and promote more thoughtful reflection and response. We no longer view read-aloud as just the time after lunch when we can get our students quiet and ready for the afternoon. We also don't worry about choosing books to read that are above their independent reading level in order to help them build their listening vocabulary. Our goals for read-aloud are much different now.

In her book *Reconsidering Read-Aloud*, Mary Lee Hahn (2002) writes, "Each book is thoughtfully chosen to support the skills the students are acquiring in their own reading, their own writing, or their own thinking and learning" (p. 3). Because sustaining comprehension and interest throughout an entire book is often a challenge for students at this age, read-aloud time is a great way to model and teach the strategies that promote persistence and stamina.

Now that we are more aware of the possibilities of read-aloud, we select books differently. We still want to choose books that represent the best in lit-

A record of the books we've read together helps us refer to them in our conversations.

We often give students time to talk to a partner during read-aloud.

erature, but we also consider the match between the book and what our students need. We no longer choose books for the entire year before school begins. How can we? We know books well, and we do think ahead of time about those that would make good read-alouds. However, we also watch and listen to our students, because when we recognize what will help them become better readers, we are in a position to choose the best books for reading aloud.

Encouraging children to talk and write or to interject a thought or a question during a read-aloud session is often unfamiliar to them. Of course, when we first decided that talk might be an important feature to add to our read-aloud time, it was new to us too! We knew that we wanted to have student-directed conversations, but we didn't realize how much patience it would take on our part. We were used to a relatively peaceful, after-lunch read-aloud, when we read and the children listened. Making changes required that we set the stage at the beginning of the year to allow thoughtful talk during read-aloud time.

For the first several weeks of school, we often choose short novels to read aloud to students. We look for novels that will not take long to read but will encourage students to think and talk about layers of meaning. Choosing several short novels instead of one longer one helps students learn the routines of read-aloud with a variety of engaging texts. By the end of the first few weeks, the children have shared several novels. These early experiences with read-aloud and the books they know in common will be important throughout the year.

Although some of what we teach during read-aloud is planned because we have anticipated what will come up in the books we read, conversations and insights are often spontaneous. Once, when students were previewing *Because of Winn-Dixie* by Kate DiCamillo for a read-aloud, they were confused by the use of the word "melancholy" on the front flap of the book. Some of the students thought that it meant "sad times" while others thought it meant "good times." They reread the sentence that used the word: "And ultimately, Opal and the preacher realize—with a little help from Winn-Dixie, of course—that while they've both tasted a bit of melancholy in their lives, they still have a whole lot to be thankful for." After rereading the sentence, many of the students noticed the word "still" and recognized that it was an important word to use when inferring the meaning of the word "melancholy" in this sentence. We didn't plan for this conversation, but we made time for it when it came up.

During read-aloud, we often stop at the end of a chapter or at some other natural stopping point and give students time to reflect and jot down their thinking. At other times, we ask students to chat with the classmates next to them before they write. Students are usually free to respond in a way that makes sense for them. However, we may ask them to respond to questions and thoughts such as:

> What new information did you learn about the character in that scene?
> Did you change your thinking at all during this chapter?
> Where do you think the author is going with this story?
> What questions do you have?
> What did the author do in his or her writing to make us feel like this?
> What would you have done if you were the character in this scene?

Figure 6.1 shows some examples of students' responses during read-aloud.

Instruction during read-aloud time is really focused chat. We choose books to read aloud that inspire children to think deeply and to respond orally during reading. Richard Allington (2002) has noted that classroom talk is critical to reading instruction: "The classroom talk we observed was more often conversational than interrogational. Teachers and students discussed ideas, concepts, hypotheses, strategies, and responses with one another" (p. 744). Read-aloud time is the perfect place to begin this type of talk. Although

---

Short Novels That Promote and Invite Great Conversations

Staying Nine by Pam Conrad
The Tiger Rising by Kate DiCamillo
Half a Moon Inn by Paul Fleischman
Stone Fox by John Reynolds Gardiner
Because of Anya by Margaret Peterson Haddix
Everything on a Waffle by Polly Horvath
Van Gogh Café by Cynthia Rylant

Strategies to Model, Teach, and Practice During Read-Aloud: Some Questions to Start Conversation

Previewing: What can you do before you start a book to help you understand it?

Visualizing: What are you picturing in your mind as you read?

Predicting: What do you think will happen next? What in the book makes you think that?

Making connections: What does this remind you of from your own life? How might that help you understand the book better?

Making literature connections: Does this remind you of anything else you've read? How might that help you when you are reading this book?

Recognizing character development: What did you learn about the character during this reading? How do you know? How is the character changing?

Sustaining comprehension: What strategies help you remember what you have read? What do you do when you start reading each day?

Noticing literary elements: What do you notice about the way the author wrote the book? What makes it effective?

Recognizing powerful language: What are the powerful words or phrases that the author used? What makes them powerful?

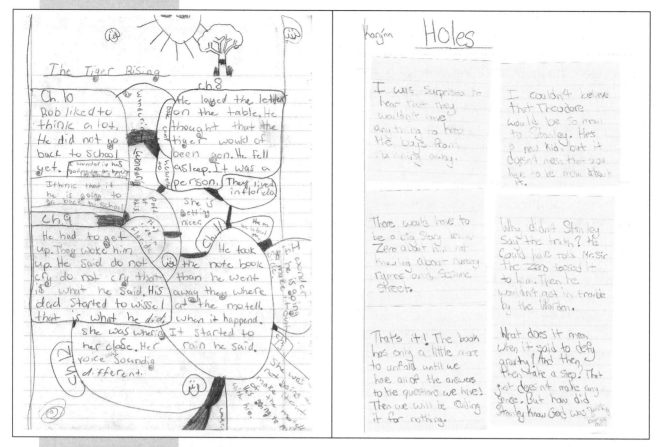

Figure 6.1 Students find many ways to respond in their reading notebooks.

students often use sticky notes or reading notebooks to record their thinking, there are no tests or paper-and-pencil responses here—only a focused discussion to address things that we feel will help move kids forward in their reading. The discussions in read-aloud provide a foundation for more thoughtful independent reading.

We used to try to align our read-aloud books with the content we were studying. We still do that when possible. For example, when we teach economics, the book *Odd Jobs* by Ellen Weiss seems a perfect fit because it ties in with our unit of study and at the same time allows us to teach skills our students need for understanding nonfiction, such as finding the most important information in the text. However, this kind of match isn't always possible. For example, there isn't always a book for read-aloud that matches reading skills students need at the time with the study of Ohio history. In that case, we wouldn't sacrifice teaching reading skills over teaching content.

When we noticed that most of the children in the class were not previewing books before reading and that this was having a negative effect on their comprehension, we spent more time previewing each read-aloud book before reading it. Franki told her students what happened when she went to

Joey Pigza Swallowed the Key

Things I know	Questions I have
I know that he is wirced. The crazyness run's through the family. He has to take special meds for his behavior. He blurt's out His Dad and his Grandma have it too.	Does he get over it. Does he became popular. Does he have to go, to the special ed school. Does his Dad come back. Does he live with his Grandmather. Does he have any freinds.

wringer
11/7/02

Prediction
I think this book is about a kid that only thinks other people are only right but not him. He has to believe in himself now that he is 10

Questions:
What is a wringer?
What's bad about a wringer?
Why is it so bad to be 10?

Prediction:
Mabey the pegion is going to stay and the guy is going to find out so he has to go to the railroad yard

Questions:
What is a railroad yard?
Why do alot of hate pegions?
Why is the kid mad

Prediction:
The kid is going to be told to do more and more but he has to fight his way out of being told what to do.

The Tiger Rising
April 18, 2003   Karinn

It is some thing like Because of Winn-Dixie. But I think it's going to be a book when people are learning how to be freinds, just like the other book. I also know that there are two people that are finding the tiger, but not together. They might meet eachother while knowing the tiger in mind. There are a lot of words that are a like in Because of Winn-Dixie and The Tiger Rising. I wasn't waiting to read The Tiger Rising at all. I would have never picked any of the books this year. The Tiger Rising isn't a bad book or any thing. I just would have never picked it.

Figure 6.2 Students preview books in a variety of ways.

see a movie without having seen a preview for the movie beforehand. Nor had she seen a commercial or an ad for the movie. As a result, she was confused for the first several minutes of the movie, trying to figure out what was going on. Just as movie previews set the stage for us to fully understand the movie, explained Franki to her class, book previews do the same for readers. (See Figure 6.2.)

Similarly, when we realized that students were not reading the chapter titles in books to help them predict and comprehend, we chose *The Toothpaste Millionaire* by Jean Merrill to read aloud. The chapter titles are descriptive and provide a clear insight on what each chapter is about. In the course of our read-aloud, as we finished each chapter, we would read the title of the next chapter and ask students to write down their predictions for the next chapter in their reading notebooks.

Many books may be used to support different skills during read-aloud. We want to keep read-aloud relaxed for the children, but we also know that we can get more mileage out of these sessions if we are thoughtful about book choice and the topics of our conversations during read-aloud time.

Books to Use in Modeling and Discussing Reading Strategies and Behaviors

Previewing a book to gain information before reading

Flying Solo by Ralph Fletcher
Stone Fox by John Reynolds Gardiner
Baby by Patricia MacLachlan
Shiloh by Phyllis Reynolds Naylor

Using the table of contents to support comprehension over time

The Pinky and Rex series by James Howe
The Toothpaste Millionaire by Jean Merrill

Making personal connections to help readers understand the text

26 Fairmont Avenue by Tomie dePaola
Fig Pudding by Ralph Fletcher

Visualizing settings and scenes that are unfamiliar

If You're Not from the Prairie by David Bouchard
The Lion, the Witch, and the Wardrobe by C. S. Lewis
Mrs. Frisby and the Rats of NIMH by Robert C. O'Brien

Understanding character development

Poppy by Avi
Because of Winn-Dixie by Kate DiCamillo
The Birthday Room by Kevin Henkes

Keeping Track of Characters During Read-Aloud

During our reading of *Holes* by Louis Sachar with fourth graders, we knew how important the relationships between the characters were for understanding the text. In this book, there are really three stories going on at once, and readers need to keep track of the characters in each story. After the first several chapters, the class created two charts. One chart listed the characters at Camp Green Lake, including each character's name, nickname, and general information. A similar chart listed the characters in the storyline about Stanley's great-grandfather. Later, when the class read the chapter telling the story of Kissin' Kate Barlow, they created a third chart listing the characters from that story. During our read-aloud sessions, we referred to the charts often to remember various characters as they reappeared in the story. The charts served as a way for the class to keep track of the characters and, later, to see the connections between characters in the three stories. Following this activity, many students found other ways to keep track of characters in their reading notebooks. (See Figure 6.3.)

Conversations During One Read-Aloud

I find other people's comments interesting. Like if it is something I have never thought of before and sometimes I can expand on that person's thinking.
     Emily

Franki decided to read *Because of Winn-Dixie* by Kate DiCamillo early one January. The class had just finished *Wringer* by Jerry Spinelli and was ready for the writing style of a different author. Franki's students were beginning to realize that there are layers of meaning in books, and she knew *Because of Winn-Dixie* would help them dig deep into the text for meaning. One of her goals was to have students pay attention to the powerful language that Kate DiCamillo uses in the book. Franki knew that the children would also bring their own ideas to their conversations about the book.

Early in the reading, Franki began to write some of the more powerful phrases from the book on chart paper. Often these phrases were used to help the group begin their talk. Students were thus made to see that another way to respond to text is to think about the most powerful lines in a story, and that the most powerful words are those that provoke strong feelings in the reader.

The students had several questions early in the book. They wondered why the author had chosen the title she had. They wondered whether or not Opal's mother would come back. They wondered why Opal called her father "the preacher." These were three major questions that students returned to throughout their reading of this text.

We referred to these character charts during our reading of *Holes*.

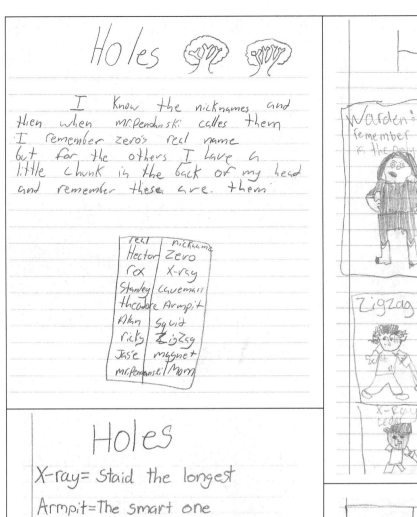

Figure 6.3 Chris, Trent, Tessa, and Ben each found a way to keep track of the characters in *Holes*.

As students wondered why the book was called *Because of Winn-Dixie*, many of the story's themes emerged in their conversations. Students did not, however, realize that they were discussing what are known as "themes": the chart they created listed "things that keep coming up in the book." The list included friendship, losing things, holding on to things you love, sorrow and sadness, and Opal's mother coming back. Each day after read-aloud, the class referred to the chart to see if these themes were still strong parts of the story.

In the beginning chapters of the book, Opal refers to her father's "turtle shell." She mentions it again a few chapters later. The students picked up on the phrase. They predicted that the image would come up again as they kept reading. The students started another chart to keep track of the lines where Opal's father was compared to a turtle in his shell.

Throughout their reading of the book, Franki listened to her students for conversations that would lead to deeper understanding and revisited them in the days that followed. By charting their ideas, students were able to think in a more focused way about the text. Although Franki didn't take control of the conversation, she helped her students move the conversations forward and modeled the kind of writing that would clarify their thinking. When Courtney changed her mind and predicted that Opal's mother would not come back, Franki pointed out that this was a change in her thinking and asked Courtney what had caused her to change her mind. Because she had recorded her thinking in her notebook, Courtney could go back and track her thinking and the way it had changed. When Kevin noticed that each chapter could be its own short story, Franki asked the class to think about what ideas held the chapters together.

Following the read-aloud, students focused on one area for written response. Brooke wrote:

> *The preacher is changing. The preacher has lost his turtle shell and he doesn't want it back. The preacher used to use it all the time. He didn't want to lose it. The preacher has let his turtle shell go and has pulled himself back together. He used to not want to talk about things that had to do with Opal's mom or something sad until Winn-Dixie gave him a smile and sneezed and changed his life. The preacher has really changed. He has made it through the dark and finally found his first bit of light. The preacher and Opal weren't connected yet. There was a missing piece and Winn-Dixie fit perfectly. They just needed someone to show them the way out of the darkness. The preacher and Opal are connected now all because of Winn-Dixie.*

Peter wrote:

> *I thought Winn-Dixie made a big change in Opal's life. Now I think it was Opal herself who made the change. Winn-Dixie helped her on the way. First of all, it was Winn-Dixie who found Gloria Dump, but it was Opal who made friends with her. And, it might be Winn-Dixie who got Opal and Miss Franny Block together, but it was Opal who got to know her. Winn-Dixie brought everyone together, but Opal kept them together.*

It was clear that these children understood the text at a deep level. Their conversations and daily jotting supported their thinking and helped them to do what most of them could not have done on their own. By providing several experiences like this throughout the year, we help our students move forward so that they could begin to read deeply on their own.

Conversations that are part of the classroom environment clarify children's thinking. As students sit side by side and talk about what they are reading, they learn about themselves and they learn from the thinking of other readers. An interactive classroom that promotes conversation can provide opportunities for our students to raise the level of their thinking, to dig deep into texts, and to grow as readers. (See Figure 6.4.)

> The Tiger Rising
>
> I think that Sistein and Rob become friends. At First when I met Sistein I thought she was like a princess and she was nice but now I know her better. I agree with Emily because on the cover Sistein is clear likz her thoughts she lets them out and doesnt keep them locked up like Rob and thats why Rob is blesy on the cover because he is not clear to some people.

Figure 6.4 Kelly understood *The Tiger Rising* at a higher level.

We take every opportunity to make connections between thinking and writing. Our students use their reading logs to record their responses to the texts they read and what they discover about their own reading. Charts generated in whole-class lessons or small-group sessions show students that writing can clarify thinking and help us understand what we read.

Conversations and writing are the foundation that supports more sophisticated reading. As our students encounter more texts, they are sup-

Students choose the tools (notebooks, sticky notes, class charts) they need during independent reading time after they've learned to use them in mini-lessons and read-aloud sessions.

ported by the conversations we have together and the thinking we generate together as we write. They become more confident and more competent in their reading.

Strategy Lesson: Sketching for Deeper Understanding

Why We Teach It: Many students are taught the strategy of visualizing before they reach the upper elementary grades. We want to support this strategy as a way for them to comprehend text, and we want to extend it by helping our students see how the text can help them to visualize. We know that writing helps our students clarify and extend their thinking. We want them to see that sketching can also help them extend their thinking and better understand what they read.

Possible Anchor Books: *Holes* by Louis Sachar and Chapter 8 of *Stanley Yelnats's Survival Guide to Camp Green Lake* by Louis Sachar.

How We Teach It: Following a read-aloud of *Holes* by Louis Sachar, we read Chapter 8, "How to Dig a Hole," from *Stanley Yelnats's Survival Guide to Camp Green Lake,* also by Louis Sachar. In this chapter, Stanley describes the steps necessary for digging a hole at Camp Green Lake. After reading the chapter together, we ask students to sketch a picture of someone at Camp Green Lake digging a hole based on Stanley's directions. We ask them to use as much information from the text as possible. When they are finished drawing, we ask them to go back into the text and highlight the phrases or sentences that are represented in their sketch. They can also label those parts on the sketch with the language from the text. (See Figure 6.5.)

Strategy Lesson: Talking About Word Choice

Why We Teach It: Students often encounter words or phrases that are used in a way that they haven't encountered before. Often these phrases are used in a poetic way that helps the reader compare one thing to another.

Possible Anchor Books: *Creatures of Earth, Sun, and Sky,* a collection of poems by Georgia Heard.

How We Teach It: Our favorite poems for teaching this lesson are from Georgia Heard's *Creatures of Earth, Sun, and Sky.* The poems in this book

Figure 6.5 Sketches based on "How to Dig a Hole."

are not difficult to read, but they are great examples to use in introducing students to descriptive language and words used in new ways. We often start with the poem "Dragonfly." After reading and enjoying the poem together, we ask students to find words that the author used in different or surprising ways. We look at each of the words and reread parts of the poem to determine what the author meant by using the word or phrase.

Follow-Up: Using Heard's poems allows us to begin to talk with our students about ways authors use words in new ways. Our students will encounter words and phrases used in unfamiliar ways in all genres. We are always on the lookout for fiction and nonfiction texts in which authors use language in interesting ways. We continue our conversation about word use throughout the year.

CHAPTER 7

Browsing and Book Choice All Year Long

My cousins, Christian and Jennifer, recommend books to me because they read a lot and they usually know what books are good.
Jordan

I choose books by the reviews, recommended books, what kind of mood I'm in . . .
Mia

We can relate to an article in one of last year's issues of *Rosie* magazine (2001) written by Janette Barber, who is a Harry Potter fanatic. She said how upset she is because she has to wait so long for the next Harry Potter book to be published and how she can't imagine life without it. She wrote, "Let me just say at this point that I think certain people, whom I will not name (the writer J. K. Rowling), are very lazy and mean and think only of themselves. What could she possibly be doing? Eating? Shopping? Taking care of her family? These things are simply unimportant stacked up against keeping the world waiting for Harry Potter V" (pp. 42–43).

We talk to our students about this article and we let them know that, as avid readers, we understand Janette Barber's impatience. We let our students know that we too wait eagerly for books to be published. We tell them about the people we rely on to make good book recommendations, and we share our strategies for choosing the books we want to read. We want our students to know what it is like to be part of a reading community whose members talk about the books they are reading, share how they choose the books they will read, and recommend books to each other.

When we first started our reading workshop, we were committed to making sure that children would spend time reading. We remember countless times when we'd see our students at the bookshelf, looking for their next book. We would worry about them being "off task" and we too often said, "Hurry up and pick a book!" Then we would wonder why they weren't able to stick with the books they had chosen to read. We realized that young readers need to learn how to browse and choose books.

When we thought about our own book shopping, we realized that we spend hours browsing in bookstores and libraries. We look at covers, read book reviews, talk to friends, read the front flaps and the first pages before choosing books. So much of the joy of reading is in finding a book that we hope to love or one that we are eager to read. We can't take that part of reading away from our students. We can't expect our students to choose books quickly if we want their choices to be thoughtful or if we want them to read deeply. We need to give them the time to choose good books and the strategies to do so. We value good book choice as much as we value other reading skills.

Book Choice Conversations Throughout the Year

They help me think about different things that I might not have thought of but other people have.
        Chris

We used to teach most of our lessons on book choice at the beginning of the school year. We believed that once we showed our students how to choose books, they'd be set for the year. But we've since realized that lessons on book choice should not be limited to the beginning of the school year, because book choice is individual and constantly changing. With each book that we read, we learn new things about ourselves as readers. We may discover a new author we love; we may find that we are less interested in our favorite author than we used to be and we aren't looking forward to that new book as eagerly as we thought we would. Our students need to know this. They also benefit from thinking about and talking about their shifting tastes as readers throughout the school year.

We make sure that our students know about people in our lives like Sally Oddi, owner of Cover to Cover, our favorite children's bookstore in Columbus, Ohio. They know that we try to shop at her store when we know that she'll be there because we depend on her knowledge about books. Our students know that we ask Sally about books we want to read. They know we go to Sally for book recommendations and that we trust her completely when we are looking for books. They also know about friends who recommend books to us.

We tell our students that we cut out book reviews from several sources and keep them handy when we go to the bookstore or library to choose a book. We keep lists of books we want to buy or borrow. Our students know that we pay attention when we hear someone talking about books. We listen to see if there is a book that we might be interested in reading. We recently attended a professional-development workshop, and as people began to enter the room and choose their seats, we noticed that several of them had books with them. As they waited for the workshop to begin, some of them took advantage of the time to read. We are often compelled to talk with someone who is reading, to ask him or her about the book or peek at the cover. We too carry a book with us wherever we go. We make a conscious effort to bring up these reading habits and behaviors in the course of our classroom conversations.

Molly Foglietti has created a bookmark to support recommendations in her third-grade classroom. On the bookmark are the words "Thought of you when I saw this book!" Molly has made several copies of the bookmark, and when she sees a book that she thinks a student of hers may enjoy, she places the bookmark in the book and places the book on the child's desk as an invitation for the student to read the book. This is a great way to support student talk around book choice. The bookmark helps Molly model the fun of making individual recommendations to other readers that she knows. She also makes the bookmarks available to her students in case they want to recommend titles to other children in the class.

We invite colleagues, parents, friends, and former students into our classroom to discuss their own taste as readers with our students. We want our students to know that different people choose different books, but we also want them to know that most readers have similar strategies for finding books they want to read. Before school vacations we talk about the kinds of books we read when we have more time. We tell our students that sometimes we have a book we've been waiting to read, so we take advantage of

Trying a New Genre

Franki talks to her students about the book *Ender's Game* by Orson Scott Card when she talks to her students about expanding the books they choose because this book changed her thinking about science fiction. Before she read *Ender's Game,* she was certain that she would not enjoy reading science fiction. A friend had recommended the Card book and told Franki that she had not enjoyed science fiction either until she read the book. Franki took her friend's word for it, fell in love with *Ender's Game,* and went on to read the whole series. This experience taught Franki that she was probably missing some great books because of the limitations she had put on her own book choice and that now she is more likely to try something different.

Relying on Recommendations

Recently, a friend suggested that Karen read *Bel Canto* by Ann Patchett. On several subsequent trips to the bookstore, Karen had picked up the book and read the blurb on the back. Every time she did so, she thought it just wasn't the book for her. Karen told her friend several times that she didn't want to read it, but her friend was persistent. She had known Karen for a long time and talked about books with her often, and she was convinced that Karen would like the book. She gave Karen a copy of the book and told her to add it to the stack of books she was going to read, hoping that she would just pick it up and start reading it. Eventually, Karen did read *Bel Canto*—and she loved it. Karen tells students that because she trusted this friend for book recommendations, she became convinced that the book would be worth reading.

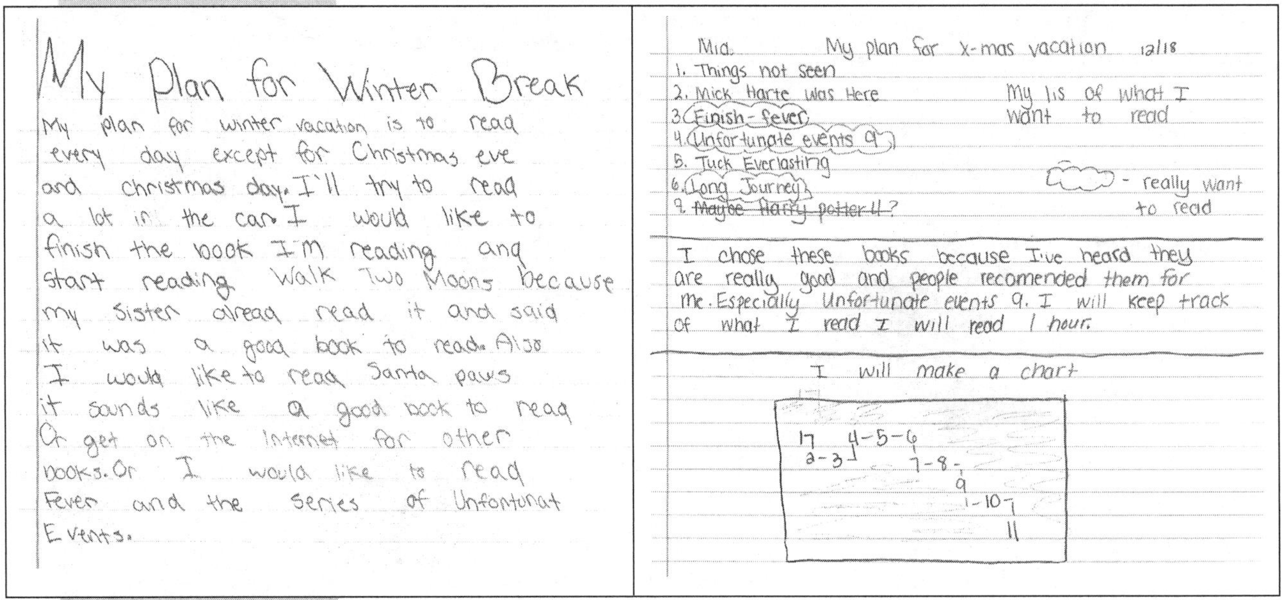

Figure 7.1 Julie and Mia plan ahead for their vacation reading.

Things We Ask Ourselves When Choosing a Book to Read

Is it part of a series I've read or that someone has read to me?
Have I read any books like this?
Did someone recommend it to me?
Do I like the subject?
Has anyone I know read it?
Have I talked to anyone who has read it?
Does the first page sound good?
Does the back or the inside flap make me want to read it?
Did I judge it by the cover without looking at the rest of the book?
Have I seen the movie?
Can I find out more about it on a website?
Is it by an author I like?
Is it a new book that I am eager to read?
Did I skim through it?
Does the title sound interesting?
Is it a best-seller or an award winner?
How old is it?
Is it a book I started a long time ago that I want to finish now?
Am I in the mood to try something new?
What genre am I in the mood for?
Am I in the mood for something short or long?
Am I in the mood for something funny or serious?
Am I in the mood for something happy or sad?
Am I in the mood for something easy or difficult?
If it is difficult, am I in the mood to work hard and stick with it?

the extra time we have at home during vacation to read it. We tell them that sometimes we save longer books to read when we'll have long stretches of reading time each day. We invite our students to use their reading notebooks to plan their own reading for holiday breaks. (See Figure 7.1.)

To keep conversations about book choice going throughout the year, we put up wall displays dedicated to book choice. We continually change and add to the display and place books in the basket by the wall. Posters on the following topics are below the chalkboard:

Book reviews
Author news
Recommendations
New books
If you liked————, you might like . . .

One class of students created a list of questions they ask themselves when choosing a new book (see sidebar). We posted this list in the same area as the posters listed above to support book choice and to remind students of great ways to choose books.

We share all of these experiences with our students so they can build their own circle of people they can turn to for book recommendations they can trust. And we make sure that these conversations happen throughout the school year. As Jackie said after one of these conversations, "It is kind of like when you ask the waiter what is good on the menu, I ask my friends about good books."

Poetry Cards

Poetry anthologies are often overwhelming to our students, so we have created Poetry Cards to help them choose poems to read. We have a wide selection of poetry anthologies on a shelf in the classroom. We choose an engaging poem from each of the anthologies to showcase for our students. We know that students find it fun to read poetry together, so we make six to eight copies of each poem and mount each copy on colored tag board. We secure the copies with a rubber band and put them in a basket on top of the poetry shelf. Children can pull out several stacks of poetry cards to read together. On the back of each card we show a copy of the book's cover. Next to the cover is the sentence "If you liked this poem, you might like the other poems in the book ——— by ———." This helps children to find a poem they like and then turn to the anthology that it came from for additional poems.

Check It Out! Circle

A Check It Out! Circle is another way to support book choice. We use this activity when we want to highlight a certain author or genre. If we notice that very few students have read a biography, for example, we will organize a Check It Out! Circle to introduce them to some biographies that we hope they will choose to read independently.

Before we begin a Check It Out! Circle, we collect the same number of books in the genre we are

Mia recommends a book that she's just finished.

Courtney chooses a poetry card from the poetry basket.

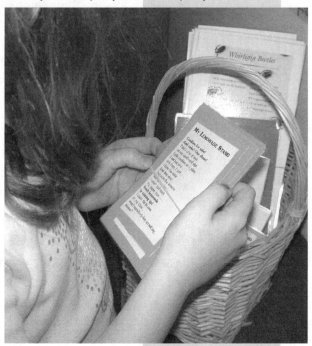

highlighting (poetry anthologies, biographies, short novels, whatever) as there are students in the class. Then we have all the children sit in a large circle on the floor. We walk around the circle, give each child a book, and ask them to silently preview their book. After just a minute, we ring a bell and have the children pass the book to the child on their right. We continue doing this until every child has had a chance to briefly look at each book. We limit the amount of time because it gives students just enough time to find something interesting, but not enough time for them to read the book. As a result, they are often eager to get their hands on the books that particularly interested them.

Following the activity, we usually ask two questions: "Which books did you see that you want to go back to during independent reading time?" and "How did you go about previewing the book in such a short time?" Both of these questions are critical to the success of Check It Out! Circles. When students mention which books they want to revisit, it reminds others of the books they've seen. A Check It Out! Circle encourages conversations about books and reminds children that book choice is unique for each reader. And when we ask students how they checked out each book in a minute or less, everyone learns new ways to preview and choose books.

Book Recommendations

I don't have a specific person who recommends books to me, but I do check out the recommendations wall.
Kelsie

Several times each year, we have days that are dedicated to book recommendations. About a week in advance, we ask students to recall a book they think others in the class would like. We encourage them to think of a book that many students may not know about. Then we ask them to prepare an informal recommendation for the book and be ready to tell the class about it. This is an easy, informal way to encourage children to recommend books to one another. They understand how much more relevant it is to share books that are not well known by classmates. Students sit in a circle with their reading notebooks open to the "Books I Want to Read" section. When they hear a classmate describe a book they think they might enjoy, they write down the title. This session usually results in some lively discussions, with children asking lots of questions. Early in the year, we ask simple questions to introduce students to the kinds of questions that can help them know whether a book would be good for them—questions like these:

Did it remind you of any other books we've read?
Who in the class do you think would enjoy it?

Strategy Lesson: Taking Recommendations from Readers Like You

Why We Teach It: Our reasons for teaching lessons on recommendations are twofold. First, we want students to learn to help each other choose books. Second, we know that students' tastes change throughout the year, so they will need ideas for new books to read.

How We Teach It: We gather four to eight students who are reading or have read a similar type of book (fantasy, for example). Before the group meets, we ask each member to choose one book in that particular genre to tell the group about. During the meeting, the students share and ask questions about the books they've brought to the table. As the facilitator of the group, we ask questions such as "Is this book like another that you've read?" and "Is there anyone in particular who you think would enjoy this book?"

Supporting Individual Choice and Reflection

When I write I can get new ideas as I write. If I'm writing about a good topic, then I can think about it the whole time I am jotting.
Karinn

It is important for our students to be reflective about their reading. This is one of the reasons we ask them to keep detailed reading logs. About four or five times each year, we specifically ask our students to use their reading logs to see what they can discover about their book choices and their reading. Early in the year, we might give them a list of questions to guide their thinking (Szymusiak and Sibberson 2001, p. 85):

What types of books have you read?
Have you tried any books that were too hard? Which ones?
Were most of the books on your reading list too hard, too easy, or just right?
How do you know when a book is just right for you?
How do you decide which books to read?
How have you changed in the way you choose books?
Is there a book that you know of that you'd like to read soon?
What is one of your favorite books in your reading log? Why?

Alternatively, we may share our reading logs to model what we noticed about our own reading. In January, for example, Franki showed her reading log to her students. She told them that she wanted to find out the kind of books she'd been reading over the last six months and to determine whether her reading was balanced. She also wanted to learn whether she read more extensively during certain months of the year. She made a transparency of the two pages in her reading log and shared them with her students. Then she gave her students time to look at their own reading logs, asking them to decide on their own what things they were curious about in their own reading. Some students made lists of what they noticed. Others created charts or graphs on certain aspects of their reading. Many noticed patterns in their reading. For example, Kelsie said she noticed "that I like to go short, short, short, long, short, short, short, long when I read." Casey said, "If I start a series, I finish it. I read a lot of the same author and then after a while I switch to another." (See Figure 7.2.)

Individual Needs

A book is just right for me if I don't quit it and time flies by.
Glen

Individual conferences often revolve around book choice. For students who need support choosing books, we hold "next read" conferences. Students often initiate this type of conference because they need some help planning their future reading. If a conference is successful, the child is usually set in

1st month

Same Author	picture	chap.	nonf.	fiction	on line	quit	poems
✓	✓			✓			
✓		✓		✓			
		✓		✓			
		✓		✓			
		✓		✓			
		✓		✓			
			✓	✓			
			✓	✓		✓	

2nd month

Same Author	picture	chap.	nonf.	fiction	on line	quit	poems
		✓		✓			
			✓	✓			✓
		✓		✓			

End month

Same Author	picture	chap.	nonf.	fiction	Online	quit	poems
✓		✓		✓			
✓		✓		✓			
✓		✓		✓			
✓							

1. It take some time for me to read a book.

2. I read books that are just right for me but I can't find to many of them.

3. I don't read many books a year.

4. I have never quit a book.

5. I have forgotten my book a couple times but I try to read something short and kind of related On the subject.

6. I have finished 8 books and I didn't notice.

7. I'm surprized that I read about 30 pages in a day

In the begging I read more picture books because I wasn't used to our chapter books but as the year went by I started likeing them. I think I just needed more time to get aqanted with the books.

What I am noticing about my reading is I read hard books then sometimes I read easy books. I have a pattern of my books because I start with hard books then easy books. Usually I am reading fiction books. When I am reading I read 10pg to 20pg a day. I am getting better at reading because im learning more in the harder books that I read. Sometimes if a book gets booring or I dont understand it I just keep reading on. These are some books that I have read so far this year.
  I read 8 books so far this year! Mostly the books that I read are not that long and usually all the that I read are sometimes short. I think I need to read Nonfiction books because I never read a nonfiction books.

Figure 7.2 Students reflect on their reading using their logs.

Kelsie begins to look for possibilities for future reading. She sorts the books into two piles: those that look good and those that don't. She fills her "next read" bag and jots down other good titles in her reader's notebook. Kelsie can add to her "next read" bag throughout the year.

his or her reading for several months. When students come to a "next read" conference, we want them to think beyond just their next book. We want them to think about the next several books as well as the ways they choose books. Before the conference, we ask students to spend some time at the bookshelves to choose eight to twelve books that look like good reads. When they come to the conference with their stack of books, we ask them to preview the books by reading the back cover and the first pages, and by looking over any other features that will help them learn as much as they can about the story. As they preview the books, they start two piles. One pile is for books that they still want to consider; the other is for books that they've decided they probably wouldn't enjoy reading after all. The books in the discard pile are returned to the shelf. We look at the remaining books together to determine which book looks like the one they want to read next. Then they choose two or three additional books to put in their "next read" bag—

Name Brooke   Date January 15, 2003

Think about your reading over the past several months.

List 3 books that you have finished and the reasons that you liked them
enough to keep reading.

Book Title   Reasons I liked it
1.

Judy Moody Gets Famous. I liked it because
2. it was funny and I like funny books.

Juny B. Jones I liked it because it was also funny
Captian Field day.
3.

Juny B. Jones I liked it because it was also funny
monster under the bed

Now, list 3 books that you quit before you were finished. What did you not
like about them? Why did you quit?

Book Title   Reasons that I didn't finish it
1.

Ruby Holler Not funny hard words.

2.
Nighty Night Mare not funny

3.
Swiss Family Robinson not funny hard words.

April 7, 2003

Brooke

I noticed that I read
alot of good mood, happy books
because I like to be in a good mood.
I read funny books like The BFG
and Mr. Popers Penguins. When read
a funny and I finnish it I am
always looking for another because
I like books that put a smile
on my face.

I like the way I am reading.
Some of my goals are to ceep reading
the way I am because it gives me
convidence to stick to my book
when there is a hard parts thats
why I have convidence because
I like the way I am reading
and at this rate I won't be quiting
any books.

Figure 7.3 In January, Franki met with
Brooke and helped her think about
her book choices. Brooke was then
able to find more books that were
good enough to finish.

simply a plastic bag that holds the books they want to read in the near future. If the child has chosen more than three or four books, he or she writes the remaining titles in his or her reading notebook in the "Books I Want to Read" section. Once the conference is over, these readers are set for a long stretch of time and will not need to look beyond their "next read" bag for the book they will begin.

We always have a few students who continue to struggle with book choice. Often these students seem excited about a book as they begin to read it but abandon it a few days later. When this happens, we have an individual conference to ask the student to reflect on his or her book choice. These students are usually eager to find a book that engages them, but they have trouble sticking with a book until the end. When we have conferences like these, we ask students to recall the names of three books they have finished over the last several months and to think about what made that book worth finishing. Then we ask them to recall three books they've abandoned and the reasons that the books weren't worth finishing. Often this helps them discover which types of books work for them, and it helps them in their future book choice. (The form we use for this is in the appendix; Figure 7.3 shows one student's completed form.)

Strategy Lesson: Using the Internet to Find Good Books

Why We Teach It: As our students grow as readers, their tastes often change. Avid readers often spend a great deal of time on-line, shopping for good books. Although this lesson can be introduced in a whole-group setting, we often use it again when we are meeting with children who are struggling with book choice. It helps them learn to find books on their own.

How We Teach It: We usually teach this lesson with the student sitting at the computer, or a group of students sitting at individual computers. If we teach it to the whole class, we often project the computer image onto a larger screen so that everyone can see it. We ask students to think about books that they have recently enjoyed or authors whose books they have read. Then we show them a variety of ways to search the Internet for other books in that genre or other books by that author. Some of our favorite websites to use in a lesson like this are:

www.kidsreads.com
www.amazon.com
www.google.com (doing a search by author or genre information)

Follow-Up: After we have visited each website with the students, we bookmark the site so that students can return to it easily. Students are then free to explore the website on their own. They often need an entire reading workshop session to explore the site so they can see what the site has to offer and remember how to use it. This is also a great time to let students know that many authors have a "New Books" section on their web pages, so students can go to author websites to see what is newly published.

Adult Readers Share Their Reading Lives

I rely on my sister because every book she tells me is good.
    Kevin

Friends and family tell me about books because they have read a lot of good books and they know what I like so they can recommend books that they think I will like.
    Kelly

In *Beyond Leveled Books* (2001), we talked about the need to extend the reading community for our students. One of our favorite traditions is to invite adult readers into the classroom to talk to our students about their lives as readers. We know that it is important for children to talk to other readers if we want them to become lifelong readers. Inviting adult readers into the classroom, however, gives students so much more than the chance to learn about other readers. Powerful conversations have resulted from the children's parents and staff members coming in to talk about their reading.

> **Book Collections That We Have Learned About**
>
> Travel books
> Little Red Riding Hood stories
> Fairy tales from a specific country or area
> Cookbooks
> Nancy Drew books
> Books about an interesting topic
> Favorite books from childhood
> Books about an interesting person
> Books about cats

The adults come to the classroom with a stack of books and describe their reading lives to the children. They talk about the books they enjoy and the books they can't wait to read. They tell our students about the behaviors and attitudes that define them as readers. Some of our best teaching comes from these conversations. Over the past few years, we have started to take notes when parents come in to talk to our students. We have found that we can build on what the parents say throughout the year. For example, Emily's mother talked about how important book reviews were in helping her choose books. We continued this line of thinking with students. Throughout the year, when we talked about book reviews, we would often start by saying, "Remember when Emily's mom came in and told us about the ways she uses book reviews?"

Jordan's mother collects books when she goes on trips. Whenever she goes to a foreign city, she finds a bookstore and buys a book about that city. She has hundreds of books about the cities she has visited. This idea started two conversations. One was about reading for information, because Jordan's mother liked to learn about the places she visited. It also started a conversation about book collections. After hearing about Jordan's mother's collection of books about different cities, we talked about one of our friends, who collects different versions of the story of Little Red Riding Hood. She has several books in English as well as in many other languages. We also told students about our friend Patty, who started a collection for each of her children of books with their names in the title. When our students extend these conversations, they might discover that their mother has all of the Nancy Drew books or that their aunt collects cookbooks from around the world.

Several mothers mentioned having read *Little House on the Prairie,* Nancy Drew, *Charlotte's Web,* and *Stuart Little.* The children were amazed that these books, popular today, were "soooo old"! This prompted a conversation about books that have become classics. We asked, "What makes a book or a series so good that it is still good fifty years later? Will the Harry Potter series become a classic?"

Many of the parents said that they did not have libraries or bookstores nearby when they were growing up. Some parents talked about the bookmobile in their community. Karýnn's mother lived outside the United States; the only books she had access to were books written in Spanish. So she learned to read in Spanish. This started conversations about access to books, where we get the books we read, and why we read.

Most adult readers had favorite authors that they mentioned. If we invite parents into the classroom early in the year, it is easy to tie this conversation into using the classroom library. We can also connect these conversations to the author baskets students use throughout the year.

The children often ask parents to name their favorite book, and not one of our visitors has ever been able to name just one. Most mentioned a few. This sparked a great conversation throughout the year about loving different books in different ways.

Several of the adult readers who came to our classroom have something they read every day. Some read the daily newspaper, the Bible, or work-related information from the Internet. This started great conversations about reading habits. Jordan's father talked to us about how he carries books with him everywhere he goes. He also told us how much he hates to shop. So whenever he goes to the mall with his wife, he brings a book. This started a conversation about the places where people read. We asked our students, "Where are some places you take books? Where are surprising places you've seen people reading?"

We keep track of the conversations that parents start with our students in the classroom. It is easy to forget what the adults talked about if we don't take notes during their visits. These visits are perfect opportunities for us to help our students to learn reading behaviors, by connecting what adult readers do and what we want our students do. We try to highlight those pieces of the conversations that are worth continuing throughout the year. (See Figure 7.4.) Listening to the adults' descriptions of their reading lives for behaviors and strategies that will help our students gives us a wonderful opportunity to encourage our students to think about their own reading.

Sometimes we take these threads and focus on them for whole-class or even whole-school exploration. For example, one year the students and teachers at Indian Run Elementary took pictures of different places where they read. They wrote captions for the pictures and hung them on a display in a busy hallway at school. Another year, students and teachers were asked to take a photo of themselves reading over the summer and to write about their summer reading. Another year, teachers reflected on their reading from childhood and wrote about that below pictures of themselves as young children. These are three easy and enjoyable ways to extend the reading community to the entire school. When we place displays like this in busy school hallways, we always notice students, parents, and teachers stopping to read

Learning from Other Readers

Conversations to Build on Throughout the Year

Jordan's mom collects books on trips.

Lots of moms read Little House, Nancy Drew, *Charlotte's Web, Stuart Little.* What makes a book so good that it becomes a classic?

Book reviews can help Emily's mom choose books.

Some adults had a bookmobile.

Moms and dads read cookbooks.

Most readers had favorite authors.

Many mentioned magazine subscriptions.

Several of them liked historical fiction.

Most of them had a hard time picking one favorite book.

Several had something that they read every day (newspaper, Bible, etc.).

Friends were important to reading
—recommended, borrow, talked about, book groups.

When Mr. Bates (our principal) is reading a novel, he doesn't want to do anything else until he finishes the book.

Many of the adult readers read work-related books and articles.

They like to read to kids.

Most had both fiction and nonfiction (topic was important).

Figure 7.4 So many conversations are started when parents and other adults talk to our students about their reading habits.

and talk about their own reading with others. Great conversations about reading have started because of these displays.

Many of our conversations about books and book choice begin in the classroom. They occur all day and in informal ways, but they are an integral part of the classroom. As our readers develop new skills and interests, it is important to continue these conversations throughout the year. Extending these talks beyond the classroom by having students interact with experienced readers enriches the experience and will help our students develop confidence in their ability to choose books for years to come.

CHAPTER 8

Reading Difficult Texts with Persistence and Stamina

I have learned not to skim the boring parts.
Trent

This book is unfolding slowly, like Holes. Even though it's short, there is lots of thinking to do. I thought it would be easy, but there's a lot of thinking involved.
Andrew

Several years ago when we were in a meeting, a teacher commented that it is often difficult to understand the struggles our students are having in reading because, as proficient readers, we understand most of what we read. We thought about that comment for a while and realized that one of the reasons why we often understand what we read as adults is that we choose our own texts.

To understand more clearly the challenges our readers face, Karen decided to see what it was like to read a more difficult text. She wanted to pay attention to what she did when faced with a challenge in her reading. She ordered a subscription to *Newsweek* magazine, thinking that it would probably contain articles that would offer her a challenge. Although she always considered herself a good reader, Karen knew that she probably read more fiction than nonfiction and had developed many strategies for reading even the most challenging works of fiction. She also had a great deal of background knowledge for the professional nonfiction she read. She wondered whether the nonfiction articles in *Newsweek* would challenge her in new ways. When she started reading *Newsweek,* Karen realized that she was struggling with nonfiction articles about political and economic issues. Her background knowledge wasn't strong enough to support her as she read. Karen knew that she could breeze through an article in *The Reading Teacher,* but she was unable to get past the first few sentences in an article about the economy in *Newsweek.*

Because Karen is a confident reader, she knew that she would be able to get through these articles, but she would have to work hard to understand them. Over time, she also found that the more articles about the economy that she read, the more her background knowledge grew and the easier the articles were to read. After a few months, she understood more clearly what the economic issues were, and she was able to approach these once-challenging articles with more understanding. She also realized that within a single issue of *Newsweek,* some articles were difficult while others were easy. Karen simply had to know what strategies helped her understand any of the articles she wanted to read.

We want our students to know that no matter how good they are as readers, they will always encounter texts that will challenge them and will find topics or genres that they find difficult. We also want them to know that readers are different—that, for example, unlike Karen, some readers find all the *Newsweek* articles easy to read because they have the skills and the background knowledge, but they find professional books about teaching reading difficult. We can learn a great deal about ourselves as readers and about what our young readers face by reading difficult texts and paying attention to our own reading strategies, skills, and behaviors.

Reading Is Thinking

We talk all year with our students about reading difficult texts, recognizing when our reading doesn't make sense, and integrating strategies that will clarify meaning. We demonstrate what we do when we struggle with content and genre that are unfamiliar to us.

We often use current issues of *Time for Kids* to teach children about reading difficult texts. Our first lessons are often simple. We ask students to find a place in the room to read the current issue, either with a friend or on their own. We give them ample time to read the entire issue. Before they go off to read, we give them each two sticky notes. We ask them to place one sticky note on the article that was the most interesting to them. The other sticky note is placed on the article that was the least interesting. When the students are finished reading, the class talks about their choices of most interesting and least interesting articles. Students are always amazed by the diversity in the selections—and they always enjoy reading and discussing the articles in *Time for Kids.*

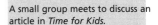
A small group meets to discuss an article in *Time for Kids.*

The following week, we pass out the next issue of *Time for Kids.* Again we ask students to read the entire issue and we give them two sticky notes, but this time we ask them to mark the article that was the easiest to understand and the article that was the hardest to understand. When they are finished, the class meets in front of the easel and we list their choices. Here is the result of one such session:

Hardest Article		Easiest Article	
Why Iraq	9	What Makes Geckos Stick	2
The New Gym	7	The New Gym	2
Spotlight	1	Gabon's Wild Plan	5
What Makes Geckos Stick	1	Cartoon of the Week	1
Gabon's Wild Plan	3	Dear TFK	1
Smashing Sister	1	9/11/02	3
		Spotlight	1
		Smashing Sister	3
		If the Slipper Fits	1

We ask students what they noticed about the list. At first, they can't get over the fact that so many articles were listed under each category. They each assume that the article they chose was the hardest. It is an eye-opener for them to see that reading difficult text is such an individual matter. They are also amazed that most articles on the hardest list also turn up on the easiest list. They say to their classmates, "How did you think that was *easy*?" or "I thought that one was so hard!" Kelsie was amazed that someone found the article "Smashing Sister" easy to read. The article was about a tennis match, and Kelsie knew nothing about tennis, so she found the piece very difficult. Karýnn was one of the students who found the article easy to read. She told the class that she watched the match on television, so the article was easy for her to understand. This conversation gave students a sense of the role background knowledge plays in reading.

After reflecting on their choices, we ask the children to think about what made an article hard or easy to understand. We listed on the board the features that they believe made the text easy or hard:

Hard	Easy
Not interested	Interested in topic
Names are hard to say	Know a lot about the topic
Lots of unknown words	Pictures to help
Long	Familiar/small words
Too much information	Enjoy topic/want to read it
Don't know anything/much at all about the topic	Short
	Want to learn about the topic
	Agree with the author's opinion

An article that seemed difficult to many students in the class was "Why Iraq." Even for those students who didn't think it was the single hardest article,

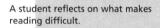

A student reflects on what makes reading difficult.

Still Learning to Read

We sit on the floor with students gathered nearby to create a comfortable feel.

all but Sam admitted that it was pretty difficult. When asked what made the article difficult to read, they were in agreement that the article was:

> Long.
> Filled with words they didn't know.
> Filled with big words.
> "Boring!"
> About a subject they didn't know much about. (Many students asked if Iraq was a person. Some wondered if Iraq was Afghanistan.)

We often use the article students find most difficult to begin to model thinking aloud with students. We put the article on a transparency so that the students can see the text and understand our reading and thinking. After we read the article, students list all of the things they have learned from it. Even though they may not understand everything in the article, they usually understand enough to start building knowledge.

One class listed the ideas they understood about the article:

> Kuwait is by Iraq.
> Saddam Hussein is leader/president.
> Saddam Hussein has broken U.N. rules repeatedly.
> They have dangerous weapons.
> They supported terrorists.
> He mistreats people.

Iraq is hiding weapons.

In 1958 the royal family was forced from power.

Iraq used to be Mesopotamia.

Iraq is a huge threat to world peace.

President Bush wants to stop them/put pressure on them/destroy weapons.

The next step was to plan weekly lessons on *Time for Kids* articles about Iraq, as it was likely that the topic would be addressed in many issues over the next several months. By using articles on the same topic, students learn how to read difficult text and build background knowledge at the same time. As time went by, students added to the list of things they understood after reading each article. The articles became easier over time as the students became more familiar with the issues. The articles and the students' list were posted on the board for several weeks so that the students could actually see how their understanding was growing.

Even after just a few articles on a theme, students begin to identify ways to work through difficult text:

- Think about our own thinking.
- Write things down in the margins.
- Go back and reread.
- Look for answers to things we don't understand.
- Put thinking together with friends.
- Use box of information and map—flip your eyes back and forth on the page.
- Read the whole sentence or paragraph to figure out what a word means.

The task of dealing with difficult text varies throughout the year. Students are asked to use high-lighters, sticky notes, two-column charts, and other strategies to identify reading that is easy and reading that is difficult for them and then to think about what behaviors they used to help them understand.

Because so many of Franki's fourth graders one year were sports fans and regularly read about sports, she decided to show them how reading about sports was difficult for her. We took an article from the *Columbus Dispatch* about the Columbus Bluejackets hockey team and put it on a transparency. Franki read it aloud with her students sitting around her. She looked up as she read to think aloud so her stu-

Teaching with News Magazines

We enjoy subscriptions to classroom magazines such as *Time for Kids, National Geographic Explorer,* and *Scholastic News.* These magazines provide great resources for teaching reading strategies for nonfiction. With each new issue of our weekly magazines, we consider the following questions when we plan lessons:

Which articles will spark interesting conversations?

Which articles might be easy/difficult for the majority of students?

Which articles will be the most/least interesting for most students?

Are there nonfiction text features in any of the articles that can be used for a mini-lesson or for small-group instruction?

Is there an article that has pictures, maps, graphs, or captions that are needed to better understand the text?

Is there an article with difficult vocabulary or an article with definitions embedded in the text?

Is there an article dealing with a topic that many students have little background knowledge about?

Is there an article that has information that is connected to a previous article students have read?

Is there an article about a topic that will most likely be addressed again in future issues?

Is there an article that would support student work in finding important information and/or summarizing information?

NOt that easy of an artical
She is reading the word carefully and if there is something she isn't sure of she has a prediction. She's trying to find out her questions. She's finding out things and rereads to get more clues on what is going on. If there's something she doesn't really know what it means but she has thoughts on what might happen. If she doesn't remember something she goes back and reads it over. Circaling things she doesn't know At the end she practically knew the whole thing.

She is circleling the things that she doesn't know what it means

She is stoping to think about the artickle

She is guessing

She is paying atenshion

She is going back to read again

She is making a line fon the things She doesn't understand

She is looking back

She is telling us what she is thinking

She does the easy stuff first

Figure 8.1 Trent and Julie kept track of Franki's reading in different ways.

dents could understand her strategies for thinking as she read. She wanted them to see the strategies she used when she got stuck in her reading. She asked her students to write down what they noticed in the Strategies section of their reading notebooks so they could talk about it later. (See Figure 8.1.) Many students were amazed at how much thinking she did as she read. Many of them wanted to jump in and explain the sports-specific terms. Franki had to make the point over and over again that she wanted to make sense of the article on her own.

After Franki finished reading the article, the class identified only two pieces of information that Franki could not make sense of without discussing it with someone who understood hockey. The students realized that although Franki pronounced many of the players' names incorrectly, she could still understand what she was reading. By watching Franki struggle through this sports article, especially one that many of the children in the class found to be easy, the students felt more comfortable talking about the struggles they were having in their own reading.

When we talk about our reading, we try to make our lessons comfortable and informal. Instead of keeping the overhead projector on the cart and sitting or standing next to it, we bring the projector down to the floor and project the text onto the easel behind us. Sitting on the floor with the children feels more informal and encourages natural conversations around text.

We want students to be part of our reading and to really understand how we make sense of texts.

Using Sticky Notes for Understanding

Years ago, when we began strategy instruction with our students, we often encouraged them to use sticky notes for different purposes. We approach our teaching a bit differently now. We use the information we get from students to begin several lessons that will help them learn strategies for understanding. In many think-aloud lessons, we use highlighters and sticky notes to help them work through text.

Students will also begin to use sticky notes for many reasons in their own reading. Brooke used them in a chapter that didn't make sense to her, marking places that didn't seem to fit in with the rest of the story. Sam used them to mark clues in the mystery he was reading, highlighting those clues that he thought might help him solve the case. Kelly was marking places in the text that she thought might help her understand what the title of the book meant. And Kelsey was writing words and phrases on her sticky notes to help her keep track of the important events in the story she was reading.

We use these students' work as examples for the rest of the class. These early conversations help all of our students see the many possibilities for highlighting and flagging text with markers and sticky notes. At the beginning of the year students may go a bit overboard with sticky notes, but we

Using sticky notes to keep track of characters.

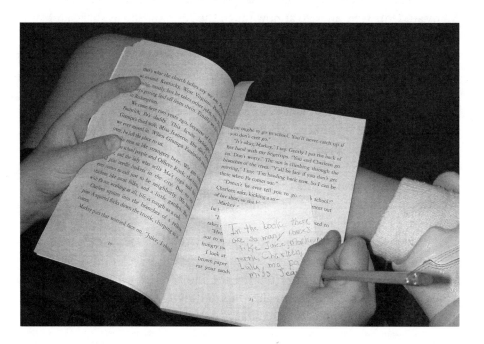

always help them identify the more useful examples, when the sticky notes helped them to understand the text more deeply.

Many students have found that using sticky notes for different reasons supports their understanding. They may design elaborate, color-coded patterns of notes, with each color used for a different purpose. If we limit children to a single strategy, they will not learn that many strategies can help them understand the text better. Late that same year, for example, a classroom conversation showed us that students saw two main reasons for using sticky notes: to help them understand the text and to help them respond to the text. They understood that both were important.

Strategy Lesson: Using Context Clues to Understand Unfamiliar Words

We repeat this lesson several times over the course of the year with a variety of genres.

Why We Teach It: Often our students come across words that they don't understand. These words are sometimes defined in the text, or there are clues in the text that can help the reader. This lesson repeated over time helps our students begin to make inferences about words in order to understand the text.

Possible Anchor Book: A great resource for this lesson is A Series of Unfortunate Events by Lemony Snickett. This author defines many unfamiliar words for the reader.

How We Teach It: We look for articles in newspapers and magazines that have many words that may be unfamiliar to our students. We are also on the lookout for articles containing words that are defined in the context of the text. We give our students a copy of the article and project a copy onto the screen using an overhead projector. We model our own thinking in the first few paragraphs of the text. We also model how we read ahead to look for clues and use photos and other features to help us. Then we let the children work independently or with a friend to continue through the article on their own. We give them one-by-three-inch sticky notes and ask them to mark any unfamiliar words they may find with a sticky note. Then we ask them to find evidence in the text to help them infer the meaning of the word and to highlight that evidence. On the sticky note, students can write a possible definition for the word.

Strategy Lesson: Monitoring Successful Reading Strategies

We repeat this lesson several times over the course of the year as our students become more sophisticated in their reading.

Why We Teach It: We want our students to monitor their own understanding of a text. As we begin to teach students various strategies, we expect them to use these strategies in their independent reading. However, we want our students to use the ones that are most helpful to them for handling a particular problem.

Possible Anchor Text: Articles in a newspaper or a student news magazine. Any book or article can be used. We prefer to use an article from our student news magazine so that students can mark and highlight if necessary.

How We Teach It: After we have worked with students on how to recognize when text is difficult for them and after we've demonstrated a variety of strategies for getting "unstuck" in their reading, we ask them to begin monitoring their own strategies. We give each student four or five arrow sticky notes. We ask them to keep these with them while they are reading and to use them to mark places where they get stuck in their reading. Then, when they use strategies to get unstuck, we ask them to write a word or two telling what they did that helped them. Following this independent work, we gather the students together to discuss their experience. We ask them to look at their arrows and see if they were usually able to understand the text after they tried a strategy. Then we ask them to see if there was one strategy that seemed to help them most often.

Textbook Reading

Knowing that many upper elementary students have little or no experience reading textbooks, we often conduct a series of reading lessons with a challenging textbook. Using a text that all students have in common helps build an anchor for reading any difficult text. We often make copies of the first chapter of one of our required textbooks. Then we adapt Cris Tovani's idea from *I Read It, but I Don't Get It* (p. 41) and give each of the students a green and a yellow highlighter. We tell them to use the green highlighter when they learn something new and to use the yellow highlighter when they are confused or when they don't completely understand what they are reading. After giving the students enough time to read and highlight the chapter, we ask them to look over their highlighted pages and be ready to talk about what made reading the textbook difficult.

A class of fourth graders listed the reasons why they found textbooks difficult to read. Textbooks are difficult because these books:

- have bigger words.
- have lots of topics on a page.
- have important information.
- are not a story.
- are nonfiction.
- make it hard to get a picture in your head as you read.
- have graphs/photos/maps and more things to look at and understand.
- don't tell you about just one thing (one page might be about the Civil War, the next about Native Americans).
- have big pages, more pages, and smaller words than other books.
- have units that are bigger than chapters in most books.
- are about topics we don't understand.
- are boring, so we get sluggish; our minds wander and we can't get into it. We know it will be slow going the whole time, with no exciting parts.
- aren't books we want to read.
- have tests, which makes them no fun to read because you have to memorize what is in them.
- are all serious, with no funny jokes.

Even though these students had very little experience with textbooks, they seemed to connect textbooks with memorization and testing. Although they identified some common difficulties in reading nonfiction generally, we noticed that many students had highlighted several places in the chapter that said "see map below" or "see graph." The students did not know what to do when they were directed somewhere else on the page. We realized that some of the features of textbooks would be very easy to teach, while others would be more difficult.

The following day, we asked students to go back to the chapter and find three to five important ideas in the chapter and to write those on sticky notes. Our goals were to help students begin to think about how to identify important information and to help us learn more about the way our students read nonfiction. The chapter they had read was on maps and globes. It introduced terms like *longitude* and *latitude* and defined different types of maps. When the students discussed the ideas that they thought were important, many marked a map of the United States that appeared in the chapter because "you have to memorize all of the states" and they marked a map of Ohio because "you have to know where the cities are." However, both maps were placed in the chapter as examples of political maps. It appeared that the students were not reading the headings and captions beside the maps, for if they had, they might have realized the true reason these maps were in the chapter.

We realized that one of the students' problems with textbooks was that they were ignoring many of the headings, bold words, and captions that are important parts of these books. So the next day, we had the class create a chart on the board listing all of the headings and bold words in the chapter. Once the students saw all these words and phrases together, they realized that the main theme of the chapter was map reading. Another problem they had was the subheadings within the chapter. Many of these were in the form of questions. The students assumed that these questions interspersed throughout the chapter were ones they were supposed to answer. These misconceptions confused them as they read, but they were able to recognize their mistakes when they saw what they'd written on the board.

Following the lesson, we had students go back to their sticky notes and decide whether the ideas they wrote were really the important information from the chapter. Many of the students realized that by not reading the captions, headings, and bold words they had found it difficult to understand the text. Many admitted that they'd breezed right over those features so they could "get it over with" faster.

We've always worked with students to help them understand the format and features of textbooks. We used to start out by asking students to look through a textbook to see what they notice. We came to realize that often children can identify the features in a textbook that can help a reader, but they don't necessarily use them while they read. Once we realized this, we were able to adjust our teaching to help our students not only identify features of textbooks but also use those features to enable them to make sense of the text.

Reading Graphs

One of the biggest challenges that upper elementary readers face is pulling together all of the pieces of information in nonfiction texts. This is always made clear to us when we conduct lessons on textbooks. A single page of nonfiction text may include charts, graphs, maps, and more. Although our students have learned to read these items by themselves, they often have a hard time figuring out how a graph, for example, might help them understand the text. We try to give our students time to learn how to read and understand how these pieces of nonfiction text work together; moreover, knowing how to read graphs is an essential skill for succeeding on standardized tests.

We like to use multiple copies of *Kidbits* by Jenny E. Tesar to teach our students the features of nonfiction text. *Kidbits* is a book filled with colorful graphs on topics of interest to kids. We have our students break into pairs for thirty or forty minutes to explore the book. Then we ask them to share two interesting things that they learned. The next day we ask them to go back to the graphs that they found most difficult or confusing and think about how to make sense of them. Then we ask them to come up with a list of ideas for reading graphs. We ask, "What do readers do to read and understand graphs?" One class came up with this list:

- Read the title.
- Look at the numbers.
- Make estimates based on the numbers on the graph.
- Check the key and/or the color code.
- Go back and forth with your eyes while you're reading the graph.
- Decide what kind of graph it is.
- Read the words that explain the graph.
- Look at the date.
- Read the labels.

Wall space provides opportunities for students' discoveries.

Even though many students can read graphs, they rarely think of graph reading as a reading skill, because it is often addressed in math. We want students to see that graph reading is a kind of *reading.* By continually going back to the question "What do you do when you read difficult text?" we can help students add to the strategies, skills, and behaviors they are learning without changing focus each week or month. These conversations are ongoing throughout the year and lead students to deeper understanding.

Encountering Unfamiliar Features

As the year progresses, different features of difficult text emerge in our conversations. One of the reasons that we need to help children become strategic readers is that we can't teach them about every feature that they may encounter in their reading. Some elements are unique to particular books. For example, Kelly approached us one day with a copy of the book she was reading. It was one of the books in A Series of Unfortunate Events by Lemony Snickett. Kelly was sure that there had been a mistake made in the printing because there were two pages that looked almost identical at the beginning of Chapter 5. We took a look and realized that the author's subject was the phenomenon of déjà vu and that he was deliberately repeating text to give his readers the feeling of déjà vu. We asked Kelly to go back and read the two

Figure 8.2 Glen added this discovery to our "Why did the author do that?" board.

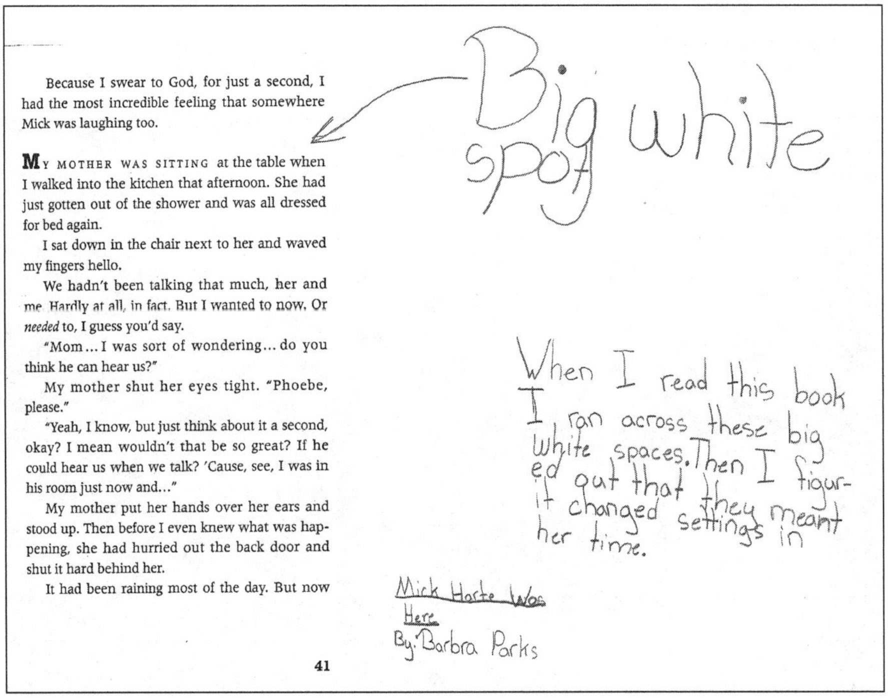

Because I swear to God, for just a second, I had the most incredible feeling that somewhere Mick was laughing too.

MY MOTHER WAS SITTING at the table when I walked into the kitchen that afternoon. She had just gotten out of the shower and was all dressed for bed again.

I sat down in the chair next to her and waved my fingers hello.

We hadn't been talking that much, her and me. Hardly at all, in fact. But I wanted to now. Or *needed* to, I guess you'd say.

"Mom... I was sort of wondering... do you think he can hear us?"

My mother shut her eyes tight. "Phoebe, please."

"Yeah, I know, but just think about it a second, okay? I mean wouldn't that be so great? If he could hear us when we talk? 'Cause, see, I was in his room just now and..."

My mother put her hands over her ears and stood up. Then before I even knew what was happening, she had hurried out the back door and shut it hard behind her.

It had been raining most of the day. But now

41

pages again and see if she could figure out "why the author did that." Kelly came back a few minutes later, excited to have figured out just how purposeful this author had been in his decision to put this feature in the book. Kelly shared her discovery with the class, and they decided to start a display entitled "Why did the author do that?"—an invitation for students to look for text features that they at first were confused by and to share them with the rest of the class. Over the next several weeks, a variety of examples appeared. Glen added a page from *Mick Harte Was Here* by Barbara Park. (See Figure 8.2.) Throughout this book, the author leaves white space between some paragraphs. Glen eventually realized that these spaces indicated a change in setting. Other students added their discoveries to the wall. Displays like this are very helpful for students as they learn how to make sense of complex text. By having samples of text hanging on the walls, students are encouraged to chat about the unique features they have noticed in their own reading. They are also more motivated to figure out puzzling features on their own.

Strategy Lesson: How Do Text Features Support the Reader?

Why We Teach It: Often students ignore many text features that are included in news articles to support readers. The children read the text from beginning to end without ever looking at the features that could help them make better sense of the information.

How We Teach It: For these lessons, we try to find two articles on the same topic. We often use a current issue of *Time for Kids* as well as a local newspaper and find a piece from each on the same topic. Then we photocopy both articles onto a large sheet of paper so that students can see both articles at the same time. We give one to each child and ask them to read and discuss with a partner which article was easier to understand and why. Most articles in *Time for Kids* have several text features that are missing in the newspaper articles. The headlines in the magazine articles are often more helpful. Photos, maps, and captions also support the reader. After several lessons like this, students begin to see how important it is to use such features.

Strategy Lesson: Building Background Knowledge

Why We Teach It: We know that background knowledge is essential for understanding text; but as students move up the grades, they will be required to read about topics for which they have little or no background knowledge. We often do a lesson like this early in a research

project or in a whole-class study of a content topic, though it can be taught at any time.

How We Teach It: We ask students to collect three to five books on the same topic (a topic of their choice) over a period of several days. We then show them a stack of our own. We hold up each book and talk about the features that we think would make the book hard for us to understand as well as the features that we think would support us. We then ask the students to look through each of their books to discover the features that may make the book difficult or easy for them. We have them jot these features on sticky notes and place them on the front of the book. Following small-group discussion of the features, we ask the students which books they plan to read first and why. After having spent a great deal of time with the books, children often will choose the book that they think will be the easiest for them. We then discuss with them the importance of building background knowledge and how reading easy texts can give them the background knowledge they need to understand more difficult texts on a given topic.

Follow-Up: As the students read their books over the course of several days or weeks, we bring the class back together to discuss what they are reading. We focus our talk on the importance of building background knowledge on your own before moving on to more difficult reading.

CHAPTER 9

Supporting Thinking with Evidence from the Text

I was thinking of something that probably wouldn't happen, but I wanted it to. Then someone said, "What are the odds of that happening?" So, I changed my thinking.
     Brooke

What do you make of the following?

When danger dares to cross my path, I stretch my majestic twelve-foot height, thrash my fearsome four-inch claws, and roar a sharp-toothed growl backed by every ounce of my one thousand pounds. But I don't do it often. Mama Bear doesn't like it when I raise my voice. She likes my teeth better when I smile . . . which makes me smile a lot. The other thing Mama isn't fond of is my big belly, and aw, she's right. A few hundred extra pounds does call for a large dose of discipline, diet, and exercise. I just don't care much for exercise. In fact, on the morning of "the Incident" I'd fixed some high-fiber oatmeal and set it on the table, hoping to get out of our morning walk. Mama sweetly thanked me . . . then insisted we hit the road and enjoy breakfast when we came back. How could I argue? She and my boy were willing to join me in my battle of the bulge, and along the way Mama generously ignored my checking the beehives for honeycomb, looking under logs for moth larvae, and grabbing treats from picnic garbage cans. Our walk went fine, but when we returned home, we found our front door ajar.

(General H. Norman Schwarzkopf, *Once Upon a Fairy Tale*, p. 41)

When you start to read this story, you may be confused about just who is telling the story. Once you think you have identified the narrator, you can go back over what you've read to find phrases that validate your thinking. But upper elementary readers are still learning how to do this—how to make inferences and predictions using evidence from the text to validate their thinking.

It is hard to teach children who want to be "right" that their thoughts, inferences, and predictions while reading often change as they discover more in the text. Children want to read the ending that they hope will happen. Despite the evidence in the text, young readers tend to hold on to their initial ideas, and comprehension often suffers as a result. As stories become more complex, initial thoughts, inferences, and predictions are less likely to be accurate. Skilled readers use what they read to support or negate their previous ideas. We want our students to be able to value such changes in thinking. We ask, "What in the book makes you think that?" to encourage them to think more deeply about what they are reading and thinking. We want our students to notice where their thinking changes and when their thoughts and predictions are incorrect. We design experiences for children to surprise them in their reading, and we teach them to watch for evidence that validates their initial reactions to the text. If we encourage and celebrate changes in thinking, rather than "correct" responses, reading improves.

Success on many of the standardized tests that are administered to children across the nation depends on inferential reasoning supported by evidence in the text. If our children are to perform well on these tests, they will need to depend on strategies for finding evidence in the text that supports their inferences and allow the evidence to change their thinking as they read.

Finding Evidence in the Text

To help students begin to use evidence in their reading, we often use the book *The Stranger* by Chris Van Allsburg. The reader must put together the clues that the author weaves through the text to figure out who the title character might be. Children often need to reread the book several times because they miss many of the author's clues during the first or second reading. When we teach this lesson, we often start by reading the book aloud to students. After the first read, most students are frustrated to find that Van Allsburg does not specifically identify the stranger. (One year, students even asked if there was a website that would tell them the answer!)

We might read this book three or four times to the same group of students, giving them a chance to find as many clues as they can. Then we ask them who they think the stranger is based on the evidence in the text. When we ask them to validate their thinking with evidence from the text, students can no longer just come up with an unsubstantiated idea or thought. They need to learn to rethink their original assumptions based on knowledge they have gained from the text. We scaffold this learning with two-column forms to track thinking. (See Figure 9.1; the form is given in the appendix.)

These conversations are often the first step in building students' reading stamina. They begin to see a new purpose for reading, and they understand that as books become more complex, reading becomes a more sophisticated process. Their job becomes a bit more challenging, but also more rewarding. They begin to see that a single reading may not be enough to fully understand a text. They begin to realize the power in rereading and rethinking.

We know that we need to do more than simply teach comprehension strategies in order for students to apply them independently. We realized early on that students aren't often aware of what works for them or when they need to stop reading to clarify meaning. They are familiar with various comprehension strategies and can discuss them with us. They can tell us they are making a connection or making an inference, but they don't always know how and when to use that strategy when reading difficult texts on their own.

We've all had students who make predictions and respond to questions without taking into account what they have learned so far from the text. One year, Meg suggested that a character had been robbed and knocked down when in fact the story clearly implied that the character had had a heart attack. When we asked Meg to explain why she thought this she said, "I just think that it happened. It could have happened." Even though Meg had nothing to substantiate her inference, she believed that readers could make their own decisions about what happens in a story. Of course, misinformation like this can change the entire message of the text.

We want to encourage our students to go back into the text to validate their thinking. We want them to realize that there are signals to be found in the text that can shape their thinking as they read, and we want them to know that they can review the text and change their thinking. Going back into the text to support thinking is something we focus on all year. We know that when students can justify their thinking through use of the text, their skills at inferring, predicting, and synthesizing are sharpened.

Figure 9.1 Kelly's two-column chart.

Who is the stranger?	What in the book makes you think that?
Father Time	I think that because the trees didnt change color when he was with them but the trees next to their home turned colors. Then I also think that because befor the frost or the winds he said see you next fall.

Different Possibilities for Headings in Two-Column Notes

- What do you know about the character?—How do you know?
- How did your thinking change?—What part of the text changed your thinking?
- What do you think will happen?—What in the text makes you think that?
- What connections do you have?—How do the connections help you understand the text better?
- Which part of the text was difficult to understand?—What did you do to help yourself?

Strategy Lesson: Understanding Alternative Perspectives

Why We Teach It: Students in the upper elementary grades often encounter texts that show differing viewpoints. We want our students to be able to weigh the evidence in the texts that they read to form their own opinions that they can support.

Possible Anchor Book: A great book for a lesson like this is *Should There Be Zoos?* by Tony Stead, a compilation of eight essays written by fourth-grade students, with each presenting an argument either for or against zoos.

How We Teach It: The idea here is to provide opportunities for students to see many perspectives on a single issue and to consider their own opinions—in this case on zoos. After reading the text, students can move into book talk groups, or they can write about their own thinking about zoos while supporting it with information presented in the book.

We keep our eye out for poetry and other short texts to help students begin to learn how critical it is to use evidence from text in their thinking. A favorite book of poetry is *When Riddles Come Rumbling: Poems to Ponder* by Rebecca Kai Dotlich. This book is filled with poems that give readers clues about the object described in the poem. For one lesson, for example, we chose a poem about a roller coaster. We copied the poem on the left half of a sheet of paper and left the right half blank so that students could record their thinking. Students struggled with the meaning of the poem, but they had fun with it.

We noticed that many students used just one word or phrase on which to base their decision about the poem, without checking to see if the entire poem fit their interpretation. For example, when one student read the word "twirl" in the poem, she decided that the subject was a washing machine, even though the rest of the poem didn't support that idea. During a later lesson, another student shared her response with the class. She was able to show that all of the evidence in the text supported her thinking. She explained how she thought through each line to see if her prediction was accurate. After that demonstration, we gave students another poem to read so they could try their hand at using the evidence in the entire text to support their thinking. (See Figure 9.2.)

When reading *The Table Where Rich People Sit* by Byrd Baylor, students naturally fall into a conversation about what it means to be rich. The text presents two perspectives of what it means to be rich. We use this book to

Top figure (Figure 9.2):

I think it's a gumbal Machine because I have evaninsed (I) is a gumbal

You put a coin in the gumbal machine

With just one coin (I)
  t
  u
  m ← Gumbals tumble out.
  b
  l
  e
  out
from a round glass world   The Gumbal
through a silver   sits on the glass
  s   spere.
  p
  o   Gumbals go though
  u   the silver
  t.   Pecher

Figure 9.2 Kevin found evidence in many places to support his thinking.

help students see another way to use evidence from the text to support their ideas, and we have them use that evidence to write a response. We give them a two-column sheet (see the form in the appendix); students decide whether the evidence they find should go in the "Yes" column (meaning "yes, the people in the book were rich") or in the "No" column ("no, they were not rich"). (See Figure 9.3.) This activity leads to interesting conversations. For example, Tessa asked Peter how he decided that the family was rich because his "Yes" column did not seem to have the most evidence. This led to a thoughtful conversation about the strength of the evidence. The children tried to determine if *more* evidence or *stronger* evidence was more important to support their thinking.

Strategy Lesson: Using Evidence in the Text to Support an Inference

Why We Teach It: Inferring from the text is a critical skill as readers become more sophisticated. Students need to use the clues that the author leaves to make sense of what they read.

Possible Anchor Book: *Once Upon a Fairy Tale: Four Favorite Stories,* a collection of one-page

Figure 9.3 Andrew collected evidence while listening to *The Table Where Rich People Sit.*

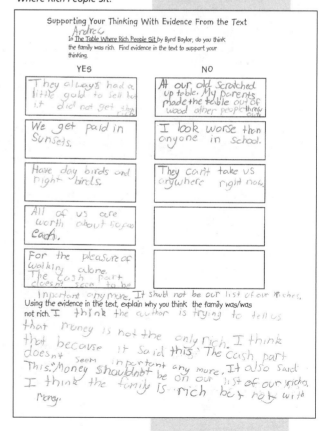

Supporting Your Thinking With Evidence From the Text
Andrew
In The Table Where Rich People Sit by Byrd Baylor, do you think the family was rich. Find evidence in the text to support your thinking.

YES	NO
They always had a little gold to sell but it did not get thir	At our old scratched up table. My parents made the table out of wood other people threw out.
We get paid in Sunsets.	I look worse than anyone in school.
Have day birds and night birds.	They can't take us anywhere right now.
All of us are worth about 100.00 Each.	
For the pleasure of walking alone. The Cash part doesn't seem to be Inportant any more. It shubl not be our list of our Riches.	

Using the evidence in the text, explain why you think the family was/was not rich. I think the author is trying to tell us that money is not the only rich. I think that because it said this: The Cash part doesn't seem inportant any more. It also said This: Money shouldnot be on our list of our riches. I think the family is rich but not with money.

Figure 9.4 Glen marked evidence in the text to determine the identity of the narrator in this excerpt from *Once Upon a Fairy Tale*.

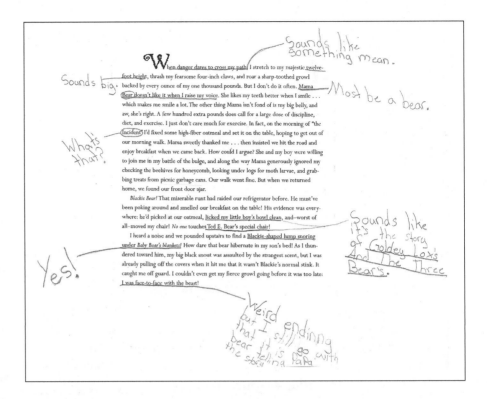

stories written from the perspective of a favorite fairy tale character. The stories are updated and humorous.

How We Teach It: We share one of the stories with our students. We ask them to infer the identity of the narrator. They look for evidence in the text to defend their thinking. They can use the evidence they have found to write a response or to talk to others in a group to determine whether their inference is correct. (See Figure 9.4.)

Follow-Up: Some of the stories are obvious and require minimal inferring. Others are quite tricky. After working through an easier story, you might try your students on the more difficult ones.

Strategy Practice: Using Evidence in the Text to Support Your Thinking

Why We Teach It: Students benefit from learning how to find evidence from the text to support their thinking in many ways. This lesson allows them to use evidence from the text to support their personal response.

Possible Anchor Book: *Odd Jobs* by Ellen Weiss. This book describes several people with unusual jobs. Each job is described in a few pages and can be read in one sitting.

How We Teach It: We share the book with students and show them photos of many of the "odd jobs" included in the book. Then we give them each a copy of the accompanying text for one of the jobs. (Our favorite is "Master Sniffer.") Before they read, we ask them to be on the lookout for words and phrases that make them think about whether or not they would like the particular job and to highlight the places that make them think they would or would not like the job. Following their reading, we ask students to write a response about whether or not they would enjoy a particular job, using the evidence they marked in the text to support their thinking. (See Figure 9.5.)

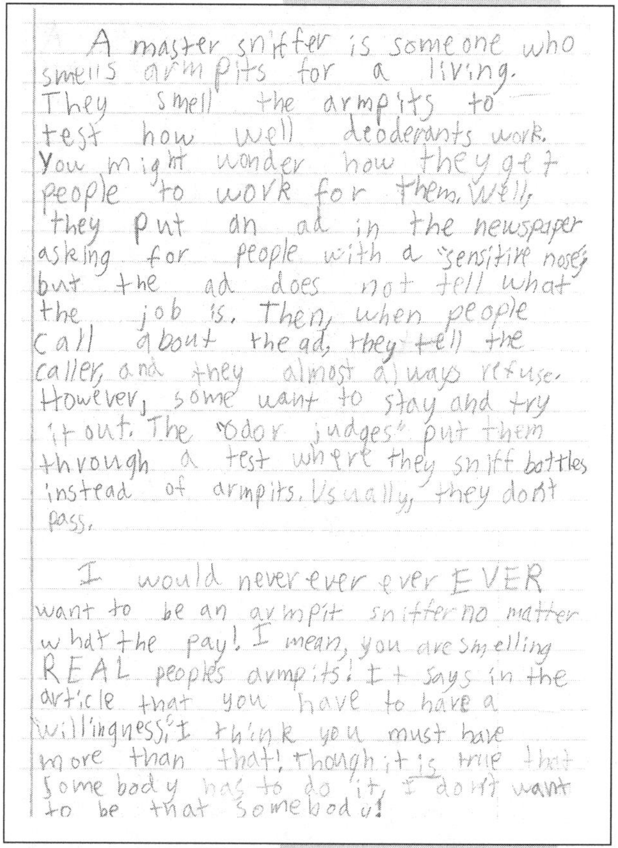

Follow-Up: As a whole class, chart all of the phrases that students marked. As you do so, sort the phrases into two columns: phrases that made us think we'd like the job and phrases that made us think we wouldn't like the job.

> A master sniffer is someone who smells armpits for a living. They smell the armpits to test how well deoderants work. You might wonder how they get people to work for them. Well, they put an ad in the newspaper asking for people with a "sensitive nose," but the ad does not tell what the job is. Then, when people call about the ad, they tell the caller, and they almost always refuse. However, some want to stay and try it out. The "odor judges" put them through a test where they sniff bottles instead of armpits. Usually, they don't pass.
>
> I would never ever ever EVER want to be an armpit sniffer no matter what the pay! I mean, you are smelling REAL people's armpits! It says in the article that you have to have a willingness. I think you must have more than that! though it is true that somebody has to do it, I don't want to be that somebody!

Figure 9.5 Peter decides he would never want to be a "Master Sniffer" after reading the description in *Odd Jobs*.

Because finding evidence in the text is a topic of conversation throughout the year, it comes up during read-aloud discussions. During a reading of *Wringer* by Jerry Spinelli, for example, students were beginning to find evidence that the main character's mother did not like the town's tradition of Pigeon Day. You can use student-initiated conversations as a way into a lesson on how they can make more informed decisions while reading. Students were accustomed to working with sticky notes, but because it was important that they keep track of their thinking over time, we created a sheet that resembled six sticky notes on a page. We gave students this sheet of "invisible" sticky notes to collect evidence that supported or went against their prediction. They used this strategy throughout the reading of *Wringer* as they collected ideas that helped them think through the text. (See Figure 9.6; a form that may be used for this activity is given in the appendix.)

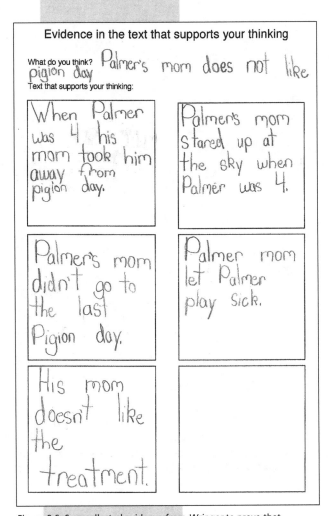

Evidence in the text that supports your thinking

What do you think? Palmer's mom does not like pigion day

Text that supports your thinking:

> When Palmer was 4 his mom took him away from pigion day.

> Palmers mom stared up at the sky when Palmer was 4.

> Palmers mom didn't go to the last Pigion day.

> Palmer mom let Palmer play sick.

> His mom doesn't like the treatment.

Figure 9.6 Sam collected evidence from *Wringer* to prove that Palmer's mother did not like Pigeon Day.

Students can also use evidence in the text to help them determine the meaning of unfamiliar words. They can learn to look for the clues the author places in the text to identify what a word might mean.

Strategy Lesson: Problem-Solving the Meaning of Unknown Words

Why We Teach It: As students encounter more difficult texts, especially content-related texts, they will continue to come across words that are unfamiliar to them. Students at this stage should be able to decode the unknown word as well as determine its meaning in order to comprehend the text.

Possible Anchor Book: *Baloney* by Jon Scieszka. This book is a picture book about an alien, Henry P. Baloney, who is in trouble for being late to school. On the inside flap of the book, we learn that not only is the book about using your imagination to get out of tight spots, but it is also about "that weird feeling you get when you are learning to read and every other word looks like it comes from outer space." Henry's very special language in the text uses words (in bold) that are conspicuously unfamiliar to readers. This is a great book to use with students because it is obvious that we wouldn't expect them to have previously seen the boldface words. At first glance, each word seems like a nonsense word. But at the end of the book is a "decoder" page. There, readers discover that each word is from a different language on earth and that each one means something very familiar.

How We Teach It: This lesson can be taught as a read-aloud with a small group, or each child can have a copy of the text for shared reading. While reading the book, we stop at each unknown word. We ask children how they would say the word. We tell them that often readers can say a word correctly without knowing what the word means. We remind students that understanding is what reading is all about. Then we ask them if they can use the context of the sentence and the pictures to make a prediction about what the word means. After each prediction, we ask them to explain their thinking and encourage them to tell how they used the context and pictures to predict the meaning. We continue

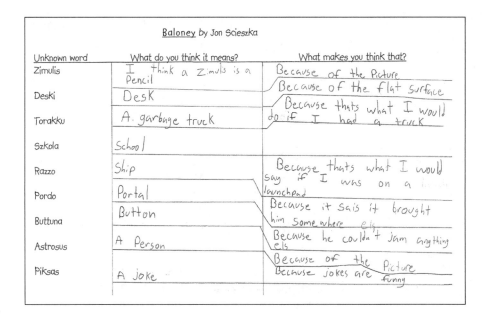

with this conversation through the entire book. They use sticky notes to record their predictions. (See Figure 9.7; a form that may be used is given in the appendix.)

Follow-Up: Make a chart of the strategies the children used when they came to a word they didn't understand. Use the glossary in the book to check the meaning of the unknown words. Go back into the text to look at the context and the pictures again to look for clues that readers may have missed the first time through.

Encourage children to write the words they don't understand in their independent reading on sticky notes. On each sticky note or on a form, they can write the unknown word, their prediction for what the word means, and the basis for their thinking.

Strategy Lesson: Using the Context of a Sentence or Paragraph to Determine the Meaning of an Unknown Word

Why We Teach It: Often, words are defined within the context of the text a child is reading. But too often, children don't realize this, and they don't pick up on the information. Using the context to help determine meaning will help them see that there are clues in the text to help us as we read.

Possible Anchor Book: *Pirate Diary: The Journal of Jake Carpenter* by Richard Platt. This book features a diary format as nine-year-old Jake

Time For Kids _Shea_

Find the article that is the most difficult for you to read. In the left column, write down the word or phrase where you notice that you are getting stuck. In the right column, write down what you did to help yourself understand the text when you realized you were stuck. _Bones from the ice age_

Where I Got Stuck	What I Did to Help Myself
ancestors	_looked for clues to support what it meant._ _I said it was a older sibling._
Buteux	_I never found out what it ment I think it ment animal. I think its a animal because it starts with a capital letter._
Rhinoceroses we see	_I did not stop at the period, so I read it again and stoped at the period._

Figure 9.8 Shea kept track of strategies he used when he got stuck.

Carpenter recounts his daily adventures on a pirate ship. The glossary and index in this book are unique. Page numbers that are underlined in the index show where words that pirates would have used are explained in the text that contains them. This makes it a great resource for this type of lesson.

How We Teach It: Because the book is in the form of a diary, daily excerpts can be used independently as single-page lessons. Using the glossary, we choose an excerpt that has one or more difficult words that are defined in the context of the text. We ask children to read the text independently and share what they think is the meaning of the unknown word. Then we have them highlight the words in the rest of the text that helped them determine the meaning. Children can do this several times with different excerpts from the book or with issues of a news magazine. (See Figure 9.8; a form for this activity, using _Time for Kids,_ may be found in the appendix.)

Follow-Up: After doing this activity several times, we have children chart the types of signals in the text that helped them realize that the word was already defined for them.

Changing Your Thinking During Reading

When I am writing, I think of new things.
Trent

Readers often change their thinking as they read. They pick up a new piece of information from the author that sometimes forces them to rethink their predictions and inferences. Children do not always realize that readers do this, and they may not always be aware when they are revising their own thinking. We help them to recognize these revisions by using short texts and a form we created that helps them track the changes in their thinking as they read and write. (Originally, we had students track their thinking on sticky notes, but they often fell off the page and got out of order, which made it difficult for stu-

Books That Encourage Going Back into the Text

The Table Where Rich People Sit by Byrd Baylor
Baseball, Snakes, and Summer Squash by Donald Graves
Ring! Yo? by Christopher Raschka
And the Dish Ran Away with the Spoon by Janet Stevenson
The Stranger by Chris Van Allsburg
The Other Side by Jacqueline Woodson

dents to see how their thinking had changed. So we created a form that works like sticky notes—only they don't fall off!) We use these invisible sticky notes only after students have had a lot of experience with sticky notes.

We often start by asking students to track the changes in their thinking with a short text. We like to use poetry because the language is often figurative, so children's initial predictions are likely to change as they reread and gain understanding. For example, we may give students a copy of Ralph Fletcher's poem "Clothesline" from his book *Ordinary Things*. We delete the title before we hand it out and ask students to use the form to track the changes in their thinking as they read and reread. (See Figure 9.9.)

Upper elementary readers have the potential to become sophisticated readers of many texts. We plan experiences to help our students learn to notice signals in the text that can clarify their understanding, and we encourage them to go deeper into the text to extend their thinking. Once they realize that authors leave clues for the reader, children begin to read in different ways.

Changing Your Thinking While Reading

Ben

At first I thought it was a clothes line because it said, two white t-shirts pinned at the waste.

Then I thought it was a human because it said, filled with air the two t-shirts puff up with sudden bodies...

But then I knew it could not be a human because it said, real and musculer which vanish when the wind dies.

But then I didn't know if it was the clothes line because it's not the main thing the clothes are the main thing.

Then I knew it couldn't be a clothes line because it said, the wind lifts the towel until it lies horizontally.

Figure 9.9 Ben changed his thinking several times while reading "Clothesline" by Ralph Fletcher.

Epilogue

Tests are . . .
A big jumble of words
Printed on paper
One hour
Two hours
Three hours later
We are trying to make
Ourselves think straighter.
But all we can do
Is sit and stumble
Head over heals
In our minds.
All we think about
Is running out of time,
Like every second
Costs us a dime.
      Emily, grade 4

Emily reminds us of the stress our children face with the high-stakes testing that is all too common in the upper elementary grades. As teachers, we know that learning and reading are much more than testing. The authors of A *Teacher's Guide to Standardized Reading Tests* (Calkins, Montgomery, and Sullivan 1998) write, "In the current educational climate, we cannot afford to ignore assessment demands that seem alien to our educational philosophy and practice. But neither should we passively acquiesce, become apathetic and let these demands take over our teaching." The writers urge us on: "This is an emergency because we all know that learning and reading are enhanced by teachers who know their students and their curriculum well and who use their knowledge of children to diversify instruction to meet their students' needs" (p. 6).

We aim to create learning communities that surround our students with a treasure of books and conversations about reading. We value what children show us about their reading lives and plan thoughtful and purposeful learning. We engage our students in reading experiences that will help them build independence and develop the sophisticated thinking and reading skills that they will need as they grow as readers. We focus our teaching on the most critical threads of learning throughout the school year. Most important, we listen to what our students tell us about their reading lives.

We began this book with a thought about reading that Courtney shared with us early in the school year:

"I've known how to read for almost four years now . . ."

Courtney reminded us that learning to read includes all that we accomplish along the way. But it is also the result of challenges that encourage us to learn new skills and strategies as we become more sophisticated readers.

One January, we asked fourth graders to think about the books that helped them as readers. We wanted them to think about those books that made the most impact on their lives as readers.

Courtney was a Harry Potter fan and had decided early in the year that there wasn't much worth reading before the next Harry Potter book was published the following summer. After talking to her mother about Nancy Drew mysteries, Courtney decided to read all of the Nancy Drew books while she waited for the Harry Potter book to arrive. So when we asked Courtney to think about the books that were most important to her, it wasn't surprising that many on her list were from the Nancy Drew series. Courtney wrote about the books that helped her become a better reader and why she felt they made an impact on her changing life as a reader.

The Mystery of the Glowing Eye *by Carolyn Keene*
This Nancy Drew book helped me because it helped me know what kind of Nancy Drew book I should read next, or what to look for to make sure my book was not boring when I read it. I thought it was boring because Nancy found nothing but puzzles and there was no action.

The Secret of Red Gate Farm *by Carolyn Keene*
This Nancy Drew book helped me because it was my favorite. It also taught me what to look for before I read a Nancy Drew to make sure it was the right kind of story for me.

The Crooked Banister *by Carolyn Keene*
This Nancy Drew book helped me because it was the first Nancy Drew book I ever read. If I had never read this book, I would never be reading the Nancy Drew series and I really like Nancy Drew.

The Secret of Shadow Ranch by Carolyn Keene
This Nancy Drew book helped me because it was the only Nancy Drew book I had a lot of difficulty with. It taught me what to do when I get stuck on something. Nancy Drews are very hard to read. Especially when Nancy is trapped. It also took me a very long time to read this book.

Wringer by Jerry Spinelli
This book by Jerry Spinelli helped me because it taught me how much thinking you have to do in books. Ever since we read that book, my reading hasn't been the same!

Courtney understood that learning to read was a journey that happens over time. She recognized that each book she read and each conversation she had with other readers could affect her reading life. Courtney was becoming a confident, reflective reader. From her reading so many Nancy Drew books, we might have worried that Courtney wasn't getting enough variety and therefore, was not growing as a reader. But when we paid close attention to what Courtney said, we realized that she knew that each book had helped her reading in a very different way. We were interested to see that one of the class read-alouds, *Wringer,* also made her list. It reminded us of how important teaching time was to Courtney. Not only was Courtney growing as a reader, but she was also able to reflect on her reading in sophisticated ways.

Later that spring, Courtney looked over her reading log and set a new goal for herself. She wrote:

I need to work on my variety. My goal is to have a variety. My old goal was to read all the Nancy Drew books, but I got tired of them and decided to read all kinds of different books. But so far I have only read Andrew Clements, Harry Potter, Nancy Drew, myths, and Junie B. Jones. I want to have a variety because I don't want to read the same kind of book over and over and then get tired of it like Nancy Drew.

Although the Nancy Drew books played a very important part in Courtney's year as a reader, Courtney also had a variety of reading experiences during read-aloud time, mini-lessons, small-group work, and content work. And that spring, Courtney told us that she was ready to move on. She understood how she was changing as a reader and set a new goal for herself. We're sure that Courtney will grow as a reader for a very long time to come.

As adult readers, we know that we learn from every book we read. Our lives as readers are shaped by the reading experiences we have, and we are continually learning how to read and expand our lives as readers. Courtney and the other young readers in our classrooms have been reading for some time. They have much to celebrate about their lives as readers. But as teachers we need to keep in mind that they still have more to learn. The children who enter our upper elementary classrooms have new journeys to travel because they are still learning to read.

Appendix: Some Useful Forms

Reading Log

_____'s Reading Log

Author	Title of Book	Date Began Date Finished	Pages

From *Still Learning to Read: Teaching Students in Grades 3–6* by Franki Sibberson and Karen Szymusiak. Copyright © 2003. Stenhouse Publishers.

Family Interview

Name _____ **Date** _____

Interview your family members. Ask them what they remember about your reading when you were young. Who read to you? What books did you love to hear over and over? What was the first book that you ever read? Ask them to tell you anything they remember about your life as a reader.

Reflecting on Reading

Name _____ **Date** _____

How would you describe yourself as a reader?

What are you currently reading?

What kinds of things do you like to read?

What kinds of things do you not like to read?

What are you going to read next?

How do you choose the books you read?

What do you do when you get stuck?

What do you do when you start to read each day?

How do you keep track of the characters in the books you are reading?

What kind of reading is easy for you?

What kind of reading is hard for you?

From *Still Learning to Read: Teaching Students in Grades 3–6* by Franki Sibberson and Karen Szymusiak. Copyright © 2003. Stenhouse Publishers.

Student Data Chart

Name	Interview	Observation	DRA	Survey	Tests	Goals

Grouping for Instruction

	Monday	Tuesday	Wednesday	Thursday	Friday
Whole Group					

Small Group

Days:
Time:
Group Members:

Days:
Time:
Group Members:

Days:
Time:
Group Members:

Days:
Time:
Group Members:

Individual Conferences

Sticking with Books

Name _____ **Date** _____

Think about your reading over the past several months.

List 3 books that you have finished and the reasons that you liked them enough to keep reading.

Book Title   Reasons I liked it

1.

2.

3.

Now, list 3 books that you quit before you were finished. What did you not like about them? Why did you quit?

Book Title   Reasons that I didn't finish it

1.

2.

3.

Two-Column Form for *The Stranger*

Who is the stranger?

What in the book makes you think that?

From *Still Learning to Read: Teaching Students in Grades 3–6* by Franki Sibberson and Karen Szymusiak. Copyright © 2003. Stenhouse Publishers.

Supporting Your Thinking with Evidence from the Text

In *The Table Where Rich People Sit* by Byrd Baylor, do you think the family was rich? Find evidence in the text to support your thinking.

Yes	No

Using the evidence in the text, explain why you think the family was/was not rich.

Evidence in the Text That Supports Your Thinking

What do you think?

Text that supports your thinking:

From *Still Learning to Read: Teaching Students in Grades 3–6* by Franki Sibberson and Karen Szymusiak. Copyright © 2003. Stenhouse Publishers.

Form for Unknown Words in *Baloney*

Baloney by Jon Scieszka

Unknown word	What do you think it means?	What makes you think that?
Zimulis		
Deski		
Torakku		
Szkola		
Razzo		
Pordo		
Buttuna		
Astrosus		
Piksas		
Giadrams		
Cucalations		
Kuningas		
Blassa		
Sighing flosser		
Fracasse		
Uyarak		
Zerplatzen		
Speelplaats		
Aamu		

Getting Stuck—*Time for Kids*

Find the article that is the most difficult for you to read. In the left column, write down the word or phrase where you notice that you are getting stuck. In the right column, write down what you did to help yourself understand the text when you realized you were stuck.

Where I got stuck   **What I did to help myself**

From *Still Learning to Read: Teaching Students in Grades 3–6* by Franki Sibberson and Karen Szymusiak. Copyright © 2003. Stenhouse Publishers.

Changing Your Thinking While Reading

References

Adoff, Arnold. 1990. *Sports Pages.* New York: HarperCollins.

Albom, Mitch. 1997. *Tuesdays with Morrie.* New York: Doubleday.

Allende, Isabel. 2002. *Portrait in Sepia.* New York: HarperCollins.

Allington, Richard. 2000. *What Really Matters for Struggling Readers: Designing Research-Based Programs.* New York: Longman.

———. 2002. "What I've Learned About Effective Reading Instruction." *Phi Delta Kappan,* June 2002, pp. 740–747.

Anderson, William. 1998. *Pioneer Girl: The Story of Laura Ingalls Wilder.* New York: HarperCollins.

Avi. 1997. *Poppy.* New York: Camelot.

———. 1999. *Poppy and Rye.* New York: Camelot.

———. 2000. *Ragweed.* New York: HarperCollins.

———. 2001a. *Ereth's Birthday.* New York: HarperCollins.

———. 2001b. *The Secret School.* New York: Harcourt.

Barber, Janette. 2001. "On Being a Harry Potter Fan." *Rosie,* August: pp. 42–43.

Baylor, Byrd. 1998. *The Table Where Rich People Sit.* New York: Aladdin Library.

Beaver, Joetta. 1997. *Developmental Reading Assessment.* Parsippany, NJ: Pearson Learning.

Borden, Louise. 2003. *Touching the Sky: The Flying Adventures of Wilbur and Orville Wright.* New York: Margaret McElderry.

Bouchard, David. 1998. *If You're Not from the Prairie.* Vancouver, BC: Raincoast Books.

Bridges, Ruby. 1999. *Through My Eyes.* New York: Scholastic.

Brisson, Pat. 1999. *The Summer My Father Was Ten.* Honesdale, PA: Boyds Mills Press.

Burleigh, Robert. 1998. *Home Run: The Story of Babe Ruth.* New York: Silver Whistle.

Calkins, Lucy. 2000. *The Art of Teaching Reading.* New York: Longman.

Calkins, Lucy, Kate Montgomery, and Donna Sullivan. 1998. *A Teacher's Guide to Standardized Reading Tests.* Portsmouth, NH: Heinemann.

Card, Orson Scott. 1994. *Ender's Game.* New York: Tor Books.

Cheripko, Jan. 1999. *Get Ready to Play Tee Ball.* Honesdale, PA: Boyds Mills Press.

Christopher, Matt. 1985. *Soccer Halfback.* Boston: Little, Brown.

———. 1998. *Center Court Sting.* Boston: Little, Brown.

Cleary, Beverly. 1983. *Dear Mr. Henshaw.* New York: William Morrow.

Clements, Rod. 1998. *Grandpa's Teeth*. New York: HarperCollins.

Cline-Ransome, Lesa, and James Ransome. 2000. *Satchel Paige*. New York: Simon & Schuster.

Conrad, Pam. 1988. *Staying Nine*. New York: HarperCollins.

Corey, Shana. 2002. *You Forgot Your Skirt, Amelia Bloomer!* New York: Scholastic.

Cranston, Patty. 1998. *Magic on Ice*. Toronto: Kids Can Press.

Creech, Sharon. 2000. *Wanderer*. New York: HarperCollins.

———. 2001. *Love That Dog*. New York: HarperCollins.

Cronin, Doreen. 2000. *Click, Clack, Moo*. New York: Simon & Schuster.

Curtis, Christopher Paul. 1995. *The Watsons Go to Birmingham—1963*. New York: Scholastic.

Dadey, Debbie. 1991. *Santa Doesn't Mop Floors*. New York: Scholastic.

———. 1995. *Pirates Don't Wear Pink Sunglasses*. New York: Little Apple.

Danziger, Paula, and Ann M. Martin. 1998. *P.S. Longer Letter Later*. New York: Scholastic.

Dawson, George, and Richard Glaubman. 2000. *Life Is So Good*. New York: Penguin Putnam.

Dee, Catherine. 1999. *Girls' Book of Wisdom*. Boston: Little, Brown.

Deedy, Carmen Agra. 1991. *Agatha's Featherbed*. Atlanta: Peachtree.

DeFelice, Cynthia. 1991. *Weasel*. New York: Camelot.

dePaola, Tomie. 1999. *26 Fairmont Avenue*. New York: Penguin Putnam.

Diamant, Anita. 1997. *The Red Tent*. New York: Picador.

DiCamillo, Kate. 2000. *Because of Winn-Dixie*. Cambridge, MA: Candlewick Press.

———. 2001. *The Tiger Rising*. Cambridge, MA: Candlewick Press.

Divakaruni, Chitra Banerjee. 2000. *Sister of My Heart*. New York: Bantam Doubleday Dell.

Dotlich, Rebecca Kai. 2001. *When Riddles Come Rumbling: Poems to Ponder*. Honesdale, PA: Boyds Mills Press.

Duthie, Christine. 1996. *True Stories: Nonfiction Literacy in the Primary Classroom*. Portland, ME: Stenhouse.

Eagen, Terry, Stan Friedman, and Mike Levine. 1993. *Macmillan Book of Baseball Stories*. New York: Simon & Schuster.

Faulkner, Matt. 2002. *Thank You, Sarah: The Woman Who Saved Thanksgiving*. New York: Simon & Schuster.

Feiffer, Jules. 1999. *Bark, George*. New York: HarperCollins.

Fleischman, Paul. 1980. *Half a Moon Inn*. New York: HarperCollins.

Fletcher, Ralph. 1995. *Fig Pudding*. New York: Clarion.

———. 1997a. *Ordinary Things*. New York: Simon & Schuster.

———. 1997b. *Spider Boy*. New York: Bantam Doubelday.

———. 1998. *Flying Solo*. New York: Clarion.

Fountas, Irene, and Gay Su Pinnell. 2001. *Guiding Readers and Writers (Grades 3–6): Teaching Comprehension, Genre, and Content Literacy*. Portsmouth, NH: Heinemann.

Fox, Mem. 2001. *Reading Magic: Why Reading Aloud to Our Children Will Change Their Lives Forever*. New York: Harcourt.

Freymann, Saxton, and Joost Elffers. 2002. *Dog Food*. New York: Scholastic.

Gantos, Jack. 1998. *Joey Pigza Swallowed the Key*. New York: HarperCollins.

Gardiner, John Reynolds. 1980. *Stone Fox*. New York: HarperCollins.

Gash, Amy. 1999. *What the Dormouse Said*. New York: Workman.

Giblin, James Cross. 2000. *The Amazing Life of Benjamin Franklin*. New York: Scholastic.

Giff, Patricia Reilly. 2002. *Pictures of Hollis Woods*. New York: Random House.

Goldenbeck, Peter. 1990. *Teammates*. New York: Harcourt Brace.

Graves, Donald. 1996. *Baseball, Snakes, and Summer Squash*. Honesdale, PA: Boyds Mills Press.

Greenfield, Eloise. 1988. *Grandpa's Face*. New York: Philomel.

———. 1997. *For the Love of the Game: Michael Jordan and Me*. New York: HarperCollins.

Gwynne, Fred. 1976. *A Chocolate Moose for Dinner*. New York: Bantam Doubleday Dell.

Haddix, Margaret Peterson. 2002. *Because of Anya*. New York: Simon & Schuster.

Hahn, Mary Lee. 2002. *Reconsidering Read-Aloud*. Portland, ME: Stenhouse.

Harvey, Stephanie. 1998. *Nonfiction Matters: Reading, Writing, and Research in Grades 3–8*. Portland, ME: Stenhouse.

Harvey, Stephanie, and Anne Goudvis. 2000. *Strategies That Work: Teaching Comprehension to Enhance Understanding*. Portland, ME: Stenhouse.

Harwayne, Shelley. 2002. "Inspiration to Begin." *Instructor,* August: p. 21.

Hawes, Jane. 2002. "Libraries Borrowing a Page from Bookstores." *Columbus Dispatch,* January 19, p. B-1.

Heard, Georgia. 1997. *Creatures of Earth, Sun, and Sky*. Honesdale, PA: Boyds Mills Press.

Henkes, Kevin. 1999. *The Birthday Room*. New York: Greenwillow.

Hepworth, Cathi. 1996. *Antics*. New York: Putnam & Grosset.

———. 1998. *Bug Off*. New York: Putnam & Grosset.

Holbrook, Sara. 2002. *Wham! It's a Poetry Jam*. Honesdale, PA: Boyds Mills Press.

Horvath, Polly. 2001. *Everything on a Waffle*. New York: Farrar, Straus and Giroux.

Howe, James. 1996. *Bunnicula*. New York: Aladdin.

James, Simon. 1999. *Ancient Rome*. New York: Scholastic.

Joyce, Susan. 1998. *Alphabet Riddles A–Z*. Columbus: Peel Productions.

Keene, Carolyn. 1961. *The Secret of Red Gate Farm*. Los Angeles: Price Stern Sloan.

———. 1971. *The Crooked Banister*. Los Angeles: Price Stern Sloan.

———. 1974. *The Mystery of the Glowing Eye*. Los Angeles: Price Stern Sloan.

———. 1980. *The Secret of Shadow Ranch*. Los Angeles: Price Stern Sloan.

Keene, Ellin, and Susan Zimmerman. 1997. *Mosaic of Thought: Teaching Comprehension in a Reader's Workshop*. Portsmouth, NH: Heinemann.

Kidd, Sue Monk. 2002. *The Secret Life of Bees*. New York: Viking Press.

Kingsolver, Barbara. 1999. *The Poisonwood Bible*. New York: Perennial.

Leedy, Loreen. 2003. *There's a Frog in My Throat*. New York: Holiday House.

Legge, David. 1995. *Bamboozled*. New York: Scholastic.

L'Engle, Madeleine. 1987. *A Wrinkle in Time*. New York: Farrar, Straus and Giroux.

Letts, Billie. 1995. *Where the Heart Is*. New York: Warner.

Lewis, C. S. 1978. *The Lion, the Witch, and the Wardrobe*. New York: HarperCollins.

Lineker, Gary. 1994. *The Young Soccer Player*. New York: Dorling Kindersley.

Lowry, Lois. 1979. *Anastasia Krupnik*. New York: Bantam Doubleday Dell.

———. 1982. *Anastasia at Your Service*. New York: Bantam Doubleday Dell.

———. 1985. *Anastasia on Her Own.* New York: Bantam Doubleday Dell.

———. 1998. *Looking Back.* Boston: Houghton Mifflin.

MacLachlan, Patricia. 1993. *Baby.* New York: Bantam Doubleday Dell.

MacMillan, Bruce. 1982. *Puniddles.* Boston: Houghton Mifflin.

Martin, Jacqueline Briggs. 1998. *Snowflake Bentley.* Boston: Houghton Mifflin.

McCall, Frances, and Patricia Keeler. 2002. *A Huge Hog Is a Big Pig: A Rhyming Word Game.* New York: Greenwillow.

McDonald, Megan. 2000. *Judy Moody.* Cambridge, MA: Candlewick.

———. 2001. *Judy Moody Gets Famous.* Cambridge, MA: Candlewick.

Meisel, Paul, and Jeanette Ryan Wall. 1995. *Games and Giggles Just for Girls.* Middleton, WI: Pleasant Company.

Merrill, Jean. 1972. *The Toothpaste Millionaire.* Boston: Houghton Mifflin.

Miles, Miska. 1972. *Annie and the Old One.* Boston: Little, Brown.

Miller, Debbie. 2002. *Reading with Meaning: Teaching Comprehension in the Primary Grades.* Portland, ME: Stenhouse.

Mochizuki, Ken. 1993. *Baseball Saved Us.* New York: Lee & Low.

Moss, Marissa. 1995. *Amelia's Notebook.* New York: Scholastic.

Naylor, Phyllis Reynolds. 1991. *Shiloh.* New York: Bantam Doubleday Dell.

O'Brien, Robert C. 1971. *Mrs. Frisby and the Rats of NIMH.* New York: Simon & Schuster.

O'Faolain, Nuala. 2001. *My Dream of You.* New York: Penguin Putnam.

Once Upon a Fairy Tale: Four Favorite Stories. 2001. New York: Penguin Putnam.

Park, Barbara. 1982. *Skinnybones.* New York: Knopf.

———. 1992. *Junie B. Jones and the Stupid Smelly Bus.* New York: Random House.

———. 1995. *Mick Harte Was Here.* New York: Knopf.

Patchett, Ann. 2002. *Bel Canto.* New York: Perennial.

Pearson, P. David, L. R. Roehler, J. A. Dole, and G. G. Duffy. 1992. "Developing Expertise in Reading Comprehension." In *What Research Has to Say About Reading Instruction,* eds. J. Samuels and A. Farstrup. Newark, DE: International Reading Association.

Platt, Richard. 2001. *Pirate Diary: The Journal of Jake Carpenter.* Cambridge, MA: Candlewick.

Quindlen, Anna. 1998. *How Reading Changed My Life.* New York: Random House.

Rappaport, Dorreen, and Lyndall Callan. 2000. *Dirt on Their Skirts: The Story of Young Women Who Won the World Championship.* New York: Penguin Putnam.

Raschka, Chris. 2000. *Ring! Yo?* New York: Dorling Kindersley.

Rathbone, Charles, ed. 1993. *Multiage Portraits: Teaching and Learning in Mixed-Age Classrooms.* Peterborough, NH: Society for Developmental Education.

Ray, Katie Wood. 2002. *What You Know by Heart: How to Develop Curriculum for Your Writing Workshop.* Portsmouth, NH: Heinemann.

Robb, Laura. 2002. "The Myth: Learn to Read/Read to Learn." *Scholastic Instructor,* May–June: pp. 23–25.

Romain, Trevor. 2002. *Jemma's Journey.* Honesdale, PA: Boyds Mills Press.

Root, Phyllis. 2000. *Kiss the Cow.* Cambridge, MA: Candlewick.

Routman, Regie. 2003. *Reading Essentials: The Specifics You Need to Teach Reading Well.* Portsmouth, NH: Heinemann.

Rowling, J. K. 1997. *Harry Potter and the Sorcerer's Stone.* New York: Scholastic.

Russo, Richard. 2001. *Empire Falls.* New York: Knopf.

Rylant, Cynthia. 1995. *Van Gogh Café.* New York: Harcourt.

Sachar, Louis. 1996. *Wayside School Gets a Little Stranger*. New York: Camelot.

———. 1998. *Holes*. New York: Farrar, Straus and Giroux.

———. 2003. *Stanley Yelnats's Survival Guide to Camp Green Lake*. New York: Random House.

Say, Allen. 1996. *Emma's Rug*. Boston: Houghton Mifflin.

———. 1998. *Stranger in the Mirror*. Boston: Houghton Mifflin.

Scieszka, Jon. 1989. *The True Story of the Three Pigs*. New York: Penguin Putnam.

———. 2001. *Baloney (Henry P.)*. New York: Penguin Putnam.

Senisi, Ellen B. 1999. *Reading Grows*. Morton Grove, IL: Albert Whitman.

Shields, Carol Diggory. 2002. *Food Fight!* Brooklyn: Handprint.

Shwartz, Ronald. 1999. *For the Love of Books*. New York: Penguin Putnam.

Spinelli, Jerry. 1997. *Wringer*. New York: HarperCollins.

Stead, Tony. 2000. *Should There Be Zoos?* New York: Mondo.

Stegner, Wallace. 1987. *Crossing to Safety*. New York: Penguin Putnam.

Stevenson, Janet. 2001. *And the Dish Ran Away with the Spoon*. San Diego: Harcourt.

Stewart, Sarah. 1995. *The Library*. New York: Farrar, Straus and Giroux.

Stine, R. L. *Scholastic* interview. Scholastic.com.

Sullivan, George. 2000. *Lewis and Clark*. New York: Scholastic.

Szymusiak, Karen, and Franki Sibberson. 2001. *Beyond Leveled Books: Supporting Transitional Readers in Grades 2–5*. Portland, ME: Stenhouse.

Tang, Greg. 2001. *Grapes of Math*. New York: Scholastic.

Taylor, Mildred. 1990. *Mississippi Bridge*. New York: Bantam Doubleday Dell.

Terban, Marvin. 1985. *Too Hot to Hoot: Funny Palindrome Riddles*. New York: Clarion.

———. 1988. *The Dove Dove: Funny Homograph Riddles*. New York: Clarion.

Tesar, Jenny E. 1999. *Kidbits*. Woodbridge, CT: Blackbirch.

Testa, Maria. 2002. *Becoming Joe DiMaggio*. Cambridge, MA: Candlewick Press.

Tolstoy, Leo. 1960. *Anna Karenina*. New York: Bantam.

Tovani, Cris. 2000. *I Read It, but I Don't Get It: Comprehension Stategies for Adolescent Readers*. Portland, ME: Stenhouse.

Van Allsburg, Chris. 1986. *The Stranger*. Boston: Houghton Mifflin.

———. 1991. *The Wretched Stone*. Boston: Houghton Mifflin.

Walton, Rick. 2002. *Brain Waves Puzzle Book*. Middleton, WI: Pleasant Company.

Weiss, Ellen. 2000. *Odd Jobs*. New York: Aladdin.

White, E. B. 1952. *Charlotte's Web*. New York: HarperCollins.

———. 1974. *Stuart Little*. New York: HarperCollins.

Wilder, Laura Ingalls. 1939. *By the Shores of the Silver Lake*. New York: Scholastic.

———. 1953. *Little House on the Prairie*. New York: HarperCollins.

Willems, Mo. 2003. *Don't Let the Pigeon Drive the Bus!* New York: Hyperion.

Williams, Vera. 2001. *Amber Was Brave, Essie Was Smart*. New York: Scholastic.

Winthrop, Elizabeth. 1986. *The Castle in the Attic*. New York: Holiday House.

Woodson, Jacqueline. 2001. *The Other Side*. New York: Penguin Putnam.

Worthy, Jo, and Misty Sailors. 2001. "That Book Isn't on My Level: Moving Beyond Text Difficulty in Personalizing Reading Choices." *The New Advocate* 14, no. 3: 229–239.

Wulffson, Don L. 1997. *The Kid Who Invented the Popsicle*. New York: Penguin Putnam.

Series Books

Avi. Poppy.
Adler, David. Cam Jansen.
Adler, David. Young Cam Jansen.
Blume, Judy. Fudge.
Danziger, Paula. Amber Brown.
Gantos, Jack. Joey Pigza.
Howe, James. Pinky and Rex.
Howe, James. Bunnicula.
Keene, Carolyn. Nancy Drew.
Levine, Gail Carson. The Princes Tales.
Lewis, C. S. Chronicles of Narnia.
Lowry, Lois. Anastasia.
McDonald, Megan. Judy Moody.
Moss, Marissa. Amelia.
Park, Barbara. Junie B. Jones.
Scieszka, Jon. Time Warp Trio.
Snicket, Lemony. A Series of Unfortunate Events.
Wilder, Laura Ingalls. Little House.